RUTH PHILLIPS

Cherries from Chauvet's Orchard

A Memoir of Provence

Red Ochre Press

First published 2011 by Red Ochre Press

Hameau des Couguieux

84410 Bedoin, France

www.RedOchrepress.com

Copyright © 2011 Ruth Phillips

Dépot Legal Juin 2011

A CIP catalog record is available for this book from the British Library
A CIP catalog record is available for this book from the Library of Congress
ISBN 978-2-9534500-1-9

Front cover painting: 'Chauvet's orchard, spring' by Julian Merrow-Smith
http://shiftinglight.com

For Louis Joseph Alassane Merrow-Smith

born Bamako, October 2010

Painting Titles

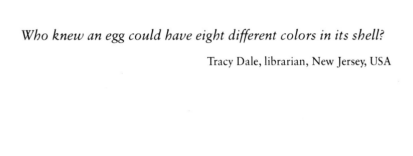

Who knew an egg could have eight different colors in its shell?

Tracy Dale, librarian, New Jersey, USA

'Far away in the heavenly abode of the great god Indra, there is a wonderful net which has been hung by some cunning artificer in such a manner that it stretches out infinitely in all directions. In accordance with the extravagant tastes of deities, the artificer has hung a single glittering jewel in each "eye"of the net, and since the net itself is infinite in dimension, the jewels are infinite in number. There hang the jewels, glittering like stars of the first magnitude, a wonderful sight to behold. If we now arbitrarily select one of these jewels for inspection and look closely at it, we will discover that in its polished surface there are reflected all the other jewels in the net, infinite in number. Not only that, but each of the jewels reflected in this one jewel is also reflecting all the other jewels, so that there is an infinite reflecting process occurring.'

Francis H. Cook,
Hua-Yen Buddhism: the Jewel Net of Indra,
Pennsylvania State University Press, 1977

Introduction

O N FEBRUARY 16, 2005, Julian Merrow-Smith painted
an oyster. It was 12 by 14 centimetres, about the size of
a postcard. A year and 362 small paintings later, an article
about the painter and his project appeared in the New York
Times. Six months after that Julian's mailing list had grown
from three to three thousand and each painting was selling
before it was even dry.

I became Julian's assistant by default. It was I who wrote
names and addresses—Hitchcockian, Irvingesque, or straight
out of Laura Ingalls Wilder—on the packages, handed them
over to Vincent at the Bedoin post office and watched as the
paintings began their journeys toward streets and towns with
overtones of cider, coyote, guitars and lox, and it was while
I was doing this that the seed for this book was planted.

In October 2008 the Guardian newspaper ran a small
headline in its Shortcuts section: 'The thousandth Postcard
from Provence could be yours... ' It felt like a milestone.
At the time I was in Lille. I was playing The Marriage of
Figaro at night and trying to write a book during the day. I
had been toying with various forms—letters, blog, memoir,
fiction—and I was bored. With me, with him, with us, and
with lavender. I wanted my story to connect to something
larger, but it refused. It was then that I had an idea. I would
write to everyone on Julian's mailing list and ask them to

tell me who they were, what their landscape was like and how the paintings fit into their lives, as prints or originals, framed or unframed, on a bookshelf, a computer screen or a wall. To my amazement, I received hundreds of replies.

In part, then, this is the story of a man who, when I married him, called himself a painter but rarely painted. A man who followed a dream and moved to Provence, and who now paints every day. More than that, however, this is a story about communities. First, a community of painters both amateur and professional who, enabled by the Internet, faced their demons, took up their brushes and started a daily painting practice. Second, a community of people who, for some reason, signed up to receive a painting every day via email from Provence. To do justice to these people and the stories they told me, I would have to compile a separate book. In this one, meanwhile, the jewels that I have plucked from them reflect, I hope, the beauty of the project, just as the project itself reflects their beauty.

Oignons Doux

*We farm in the San Joaquin Valley of California and this is
one of our crops. The painting that I purchased—Oignons
Doux - was timed to arrive with the harvest of our own
onions.*

Janet Thompson, Buttonwillow, California, USA

JULIAN STRUGGLED UP THE HILL to his rented studio in
the village of Crillon le Brave. When he first arrived in
France, he would have nipped up in third gear but now, in
his early forties and somewhat portlier, he was down to first
and straining. Tied to the back of his bike were three bottles
of Badoit and a five-litre box of *vin de pays*, and out of his
panniers poked a bunch of paintbrushes and a baguette,
both nubbin ends of which had been eaten. Inside the left
pannier were three carefully chosen onions, two of which he
intended to paint and one of which he would use to make a
potato curry later that day.

Letting the bike fall against the curb, Julian opened the
front door to the studio and checked the post. This consisted
of two envelopes: a gentle reminder of the three months'
rent still due and an invitation from the local town hall to
show his landscapes in a street festival three villages away. He
ignored the first, believing it to be the privilege of the artist

3

to pay his rent when he is moved to do so, and considered the second. Then he crumpled them both into a ball and threw them on the pile of papers by the heavy front door. He pulled his bicycle inside, propped it against several unfinished canvasses and, humming the Lion's song from The Wizard of Oz, climbed the staircase to the studio in which he had lived alone for six years.

Crillon was a dreamy place perched high above vineyards, olive groves and cherry orchards, with a honey-coloured stone arch, cobbled streets, a well and a church spire. In season, it bulged with Parisians, Belgians, Americans and Swiss whose second homes creaked open after eight months of being battered and frozen by the mistral. Garages became holiday apartments bordering swimming pools, and barns became bed and breakfasts. Children played in the road. Cameras clicked and cicadas gossiped. Swifts reeled in the sky and Julian's social calendar buzzed with invitations, his Botticelli curls having charmed many of the ladies *d'un certain âge*. Out of season, however, vineyards turned to rows of gnarled fists. Wood smoke and the smell of stewing boar filled the air, and the few remaining villagers kept mostly to themselves as peace descended once more on his adopted home in Provence.

The house itself, though next to the arch and opposite the well, was not beautiful. It was partly renovated in a style favoured by the locals that involved ripping out as many of the original features as possible and replacing them with what was believed to be sturdier stuff. In this case, a grey concrete render replaced a lime façade and gold fleck tile the original terracotta floor tiles called *tomettes*. Fortunately, the renovation was incomplete, and the beautiful plaster spiral staircase and windows with their wooden frames and lead panes remained intact.

The original layout of the interior was odd, even inhospitable. The ground floor was a single room with cold, resonant, busy concrete tiles. Here Julian hung a collection of his still lifes and landscapes. Since the front door was always open passers-by, lured by a menacing portrait in the window, could peruse the paintings at their leisure. He called this room the gallery.

Branching off the staircase was the first floor, also only one room, a kitchen/dining room. This was the room where Julian cooked, ate and painted. A room in which turps and jam jars, linen canvas and linen napkins, basting and painting brushes, and tubes of anchovy paste and titanium white were all mixed up. A room of clutter and toil from which, when Julian fancied a peaceful moment al fresco, he had to escape downstairs to sit on the sunny step of the empty house opposite. On the second floor were two small bedrooms and a bathroom with orange hula-hoop wallpaper.

That was it, apart from the mysterious fourth floor. This seemed, when Julian peeped up the remaining curl of the staircase, to consist of a spacious double attic crammed with travelling cases, suits and ball gowns. Its beams, sunset-tinted floor tiles and lime plaster walls were still untampered with. It boasted sweeping views south over the roofs and orchards and across toward Avignon, and Julian longed to expand into it. However, a tatty rope drawn across the top of the staircase indicated that it was out of bounds, and so he made do with the one view he did have to the north, the one from the bathroom window. A postcard-sized view of the Mont Ventoux.

Throwing the panniers down in the kitchen, Julian tripped over an old pomegranate to the computer and glanced at his email for the sixteenth time that day. Sun almost obliterated the text on the screen but this time he thought he could discern something unusual amid the spam.

To: jms@provenceart.fr
From: hank@t-aft.com
Date: May 14, 1999
Subject: commission

He squinted at the subject. Leaning back in the chair, he looked away from the screen and out past the pink fluff of the tamarisk tree to the blue hills bleeding into the morning sky. In the walled garden opposite, Madame Bellon, in her floral print housecoat, was bending down to water the plants. Ducking from view, he breathed in the pungent smells of her Sunday lunch and of thyme after rain, and let his imagination roam. What could this commission be worth, he wondered. A week in a Cork Street gallery? A case of Chateau Rayas? At least a new wheel for his bike? Like any artist, Julian longed to paint what moved him. Blocks of barns punctuated by cypresses, telegraph poles dividing orchards like bar lines, a bare buttress, the odd bulge of a quince, a blotchy cloudscape. An onion. However, he knew that when he did receive a commission, which was rare, it never gave him free rein. He prepared himself for the worst: a month painting rows of lavender or an unknown woman reclining in a poppy field or drinking rosé on the terrace of her *mas provençal*.

He turned back to the bondi blue Mac and read the email. So far, the request was normal: Hank Taft wanted him to paint his grandmother's house on Erland Road, Stony Brook, Long Island. In summer. However, with the request came a series of photographs. These consisted of three black-and-white elevations of a Georgian colonial house, its surrounding flowerbeds so deep in snow that he could not see where they ended and the weatherboard began. A row of small trees with bare branches masked the shape of the porch. The shutters were closed and there was no sign of a door. At the bottom of the drive a red metal arm poked out of what must have been, underneath its snowy bonnet, one of those traditional mailboxes Julian had seen in films. Hoping to find something to work with, he clicked to enlarge the images and stared at the computer. He got up, took a beaker from the shelf and, never tiring of the luxury of wine on tap, pressed the button of the bag-in-box. I've been offered a big commission, he said to himself, glancing at the clock. After all it is almost lunchtime. And I deserve a treat. He returned to the screen. Clicking again and again, he watched as the white landscape was transformed into an abstract patchwork of pixels. Then he clicked Reply. Shame about the onions, he thought, as he agreed to do the work. Tomorrow, perhaps.

I have a number of Julian's paintings—pieces I've accumu-lated over the years, and in very different circumstances. Sadly, I don't have anything of his from our year at Banbury, where we first met on a foundation course back in 1977, but I do have a vivid memory of a painting from that time. It was (funnily enough, given the way the painting a day thing has evolved) a small still life of some oranges; a watercolour, and I remember being very struck by it, and seeing how unlike my own work it was. Put simply, his picture was alive. I was always impressed by Julian's gift; it was something of an education in itself for me, just seeing someone who lived so much through their eyes/ hands. It helped me see what I wasn't.

Anyway, fast forward to probably 1995-ish (Julian would remember better than I) and Julian was going through this very unhappy relationship which involved

*him actually leaving his Lewisham apartment to his part-
ner (the apartment he owned) and moving into some dump
or other. It was there that I think he really started painting
again, after what had probably been years of not painting. I have a small self-portrait he did in that dump. It's
very moody, very good; a study more than a fully realized
painting, but tremendously evocative. It was with that little
painting that my small collection began. It's not with me
here in Los Angeles, but as I write this, and think about
these things, I wish it were.*

*Not so long after this brief exile and intense bout of
self-portraiture, Julian gave me an exuberant still life of
some quinces. I think it was perhaps a birthday present.
There is also a landscape I bought, which I remember
seeing for the first time after coming in from a long walk
with my wife. Julian had been picking cèpes and had them
finely sliced and balanced over a radiator on a piece of
wire or coat hanger wire to dry (very Julian, this—food
and painting in the same room).*

*But the keystone of my collection is a still life of
some yellow onions. This did make its way to America
and hangs as the center piece in our living room. It is perhaps 18 by 12 , oil on canvas. I had it in a beautiful frame
that I made back in France, using a technique I learned
from Julian, but rather than carry it in my luggage, I left
that frame in storage. Here, the picture is in a pleasant
enough faux-battered, pale, bird's-eye maple veneer frame.
I love the painting itself, but beyond that it carries a lot
of memories for me, a lot of associations.*

*The onions are in a cupboard which was/is in the
village house that became Julian's studio for a number
of years. This house was very odd—much smaller on the
inside than out, largely because of the thickness of the*

walls, but also because a large part of the house was this clunky staircase that grew up through the middle of it like a too big tree. The room he painted the onions in was off this staircase to the right on the second floor. The cupboard was by the tall narrow window giving onto the narrow street. It was a perfect provençal cupboard with plaster notches for the uneven shelves.

Julian eventually did most of his painting on the other side of the staircase—a kitchen which became this extraordinary paint-spattered shithole. That I loved. There were always food-encrusted casseroles next to cheese rinds, and chaotic palettes, including a big glass palette glistening with tube-turds. I remember mouldering still-life set-ups. I remember also box wine. There was a local vintner (the mayor of Crillon, I think) who made this terrific vin de table, which was, as I remember it, about ten francs a box. We drank gallons of it. Julian did some wonderful work in that kitchen—including a fabulous self-portrait with a little white hat, and he did the onions—on the other side of the stairs, and very early on, probably a few weeks after he'd moved in.

I'm lying on the sofa in our living room in Santa Monica as I write this. The Santa Ana winds are blowing in the palm trees and it will be too warm to sleep with a blanket tonight. This room is pleasantly furnished, and the painting, with its subdued browns, yellows and silvery greens, fits perfectly as a decorative item. I'm sure that's how most people see it when they come in here. But for me, it is of course quite different. When I look at it, it's hard not to think of that slightly chilly room, and that cramped village house that my friend had come to live and paint in. He had nothing at that time, or nothing much anyway. He had rented his London place, I think, to cover the mortgage, and was basically trying to come up with some way to make a living. He didn't have a car, and was making do with a bicycle he borrowed from me. He became very fit riding that bike up and down. It was a terrible bike. It had a dynamo that drove the lights. One night, returning from town with bottles of mineral water on the back of the bike he got lost in the dark, and had to turn the bike over and whizz the pedals round to see his map. This was the life he was living when he painted the onions I have on my wall. The onions themselves are long gone of course, as is the year in which he painted them, and the life we shared at that time. I was living a couple of miles way in an old farmhouse, writing novels, trying to stay warm through the long provençal winters, very happy for the most part. Julian is currently struggling through another winter, still painting onions (and other vegetables) just a few miles from where my painting was done. I look forward to living nearby again, which I will some day; I look forward to looking over his shoulder.

Gary Humphreys, writer, Dieulefit, France

Pale Blue Iris

THE GARDEN ACROSS THE STREET from the studio in Crillon le Brave dripped with passion flowers. It was bordered by lavender in summer and lily of the valley in spring. The fronds of an exotic tree—the name of which only Julian's mother once knew—wove a verdant mesh through which the light shifted, creating patterns on the stone table where Julian took his morning coffee. Most mornings he and his landlady, Ginette Bellon, would chat a while she tended her flowers, then fall to comfortable silence, preferring the sound of the cicadas and the dribble of her watering can.

Ginette was a woman of untiring patience; Julian never paid his rent on time and she never complained. Perhaps patience came from long experience with the vagaries of nature that influenced the crops and changed one's fortune; in any case she seemed happy with the arrangement. *Monsieur l'artiste* was impeccable and he paid up when he wanted. Besides, Madame Bellon had more pressing problems. Her husband, Marcel, was in the early stages of Alzheimer's and would often get lost, floating up the cobbled streets, wandering through open doors and offering up the story of his youth as a waiter in a café to anyone who would listen.

One day Marcel shuffled into our hallway. His white hair was in disarray, his shirt was open right to the waist of his oversize trousers, and he was hugging armfuls of reeds and bearded irises to his bare chest.

'Where is my wife?' he pleaded. 'I have flowers for her.'

I looked at the clumps of earth clinging to the flora he had wrenched from the nearby banks. I was still in awe of the fact that irises grew wild and I treated them with reverence, picking only the occasional stem for a slim vase. That one, I would think, behind the reeds and low down on the bank, surely that one would not be missed...?

'Monsieur,' said Julian, 'your wife lives next door now.'

'But this is my home and I have flowers for my beautiful wife.'

'Yes, Monsieur, I know. You used to lived here—'

'—when I was a *garçon de café*.'

'Yes, when you were a young man. Now, Monsieur,' Julian said, taking his arm. 'I shall take you to your beautiful wife.'

'I have flowers...'

'Yes, I can see you do. They are lovely.'

'But aren't you my wife?' Marcel spun round on his heels, and looked at me. Dribble gathered at the corner of his mouth.

'No, Monsieur, I am afraid I am not. Your wife is next door waiting for you.'

Marcel shook his stalks at me before he allowed Julian to guide him out of our house and toward his.

Ginette stood in the doorway. She took the torn flowers in her arms and kissed her husband. 'Thank you for bringing him home. You know your house used to be his home when he was a...'

'...*garçon de café*?'

'Yes. Thank you. He doesn't quite... Thank you. You have been impeccable.'

Death of Blue

1

Eyes open
after four days of fevered sleep
a crown of candles
burns on the dresser
twelve blue iris
incandescent
in the morning light seemed
a sign of something
a gift from the world
unasked for
unmortgaged now
with wild
abandoned wings they fly
and settle like
bright swallows
around the room
send a message I beg
we are!
we are!
they sing

2

Where does one find
a word
for such a blue
this iris-colour that exists
in dreams
where is the word
for flesh of seraphim
luminous as a child's eyes

would melt between human fingers
tissue of sky of star
of this earth and not of this earth
o white despair

3
Irises begin to darken
the way eyes do
in certain moods
in certain light
their yellow centres turn
to tarnished gold
they do not lose their petals
as other flowers
but curl back
into themselves
to the place
before they were born
withdrawing
all the blue
from the world

from The Weight of Irises by Nicolette Stasko

House with Lavender Field

I have four small children, Will (5), Violet (4), Delilah (2), Charlie (8 months). When everything around here is crazy and children are screaming and the house is a mess, I open up Postcard from Provence and I share the image with them.

Clair Molony, interior designer, Maywood, Illinois, USA

ONE DAY THE QUIET TIMES in Crillon le Brave came to an abrupt end. One day Jacques and Yvette Grouiller moved into the empty house opposite.

The Grouillers were angry. They were born in the village and they had watched, dismayed, as it was transformed from a hamlet for peasants with a small bakery into a heartless museum for up-market tourists. They had seen the stone houses at the top of the hill turn, one by one, into wings of a Relais Château hotel in front of which Ray-Bans and Christian Diors were helped out of BMWs by liveried doormen on to the *tomettes authentiques* of the entrance hall.

Clearly not enamoured of newcomers in their village, especially not foreign ones, Jacques encouraged his terrier to leave souvenirs on our doorstep on their daily waddle round the village. He blacked out the parking space opposite his house in the middle of the night and then kept vigil, barking like a bulldog if a car even sniffed at the possibility of stopping there. If it did stop, he might consider plunging a nail into its tyre. This was not good for Julian's business. Worst of all, from a stone bench underneath the arch Jacques held forth in a booming voice all day, every day, his beefy head turning left and right in the folds of its axis. His harangue started with the dustbin men at six and ended when, close to midnight, he growled his last goodbye of the night to the bistro owner on her way home. Then he gathered his forty pots of geraniums, shut them in his garage, made his sloppy ablutions, and fell into a hoarse sleep. Unfortunately for us, both their bedroom and their bathroom overlooked our garden.

'Try to think yourself into a Pagnol novel,' Julian said as he hung lanterns from the tamarisk tree and placed church candles on the table. It was the summer of 2003. As usual, he had prepared a feast, and as usual it was accompanied by Yvette whining and Jacques pissing, belching and farting.

'*Putain!*'

Yvette had thrown open the shutters. The Provençal -ing on the ending of the word for whore stung hard.

Julian presented the food. A fillet of sea bass with perfect griddle marks and a scattering of fennel picked from a nearby hedgerow. There were caramelized carrots, baby *la ratte* potatoes and a garnish of roasted tomatoes that had made a brief appearance in a painting that afternoon. Drizzled over the bass was a delicate sauce based on a saffron fish stock that Julian had preferred making to finishing the tomato painting. Yvette banged the shutters closed and someone creaked the garden gate open.

'Am I disturbing you?' A handsome woman, tanned and lightly made up, was standing in front of us. 'It's just that I saw...' Julian and I could hear the rest of her party in the street discussing what they were going to eat. 'Have the risotto then?' said one. 'But I had the risotto the last two nights,' said another.

'My husband,' said the woman, 'and friends and I— we're from Ojai—were on our way to dinner at that cute little place down the street...?'

'Le Vieux Four. Did you need directions?'

'Oh no, I don't need directions, but I do need that lavender painting...'

Julian and the woman discussed a price. Julian offered her a discount for cash. She said she only had a credit card. He gave her the discount anyway, took her details, filled in an online form and handed over the painting. The woman seemed delighted and left.

'*Connasse!*' Yvette screamed.

'*Vous êtes une pomme de terre avec le visage d'un cochon d'Inde,*' I said under my breath.

'What?' said Julian.

'She called me a bitch. I called her a potato with the face of a guinea pig.'

Julian looked at his watch. 'Look, Ruthie. You have to listen for the romance, ok? Instead of their bodily sounds, try hearing Verdi's soundtrack in the background. When you hear his voice listen to the vings, vangs, and pings as if it were Jean de Florette himself calling to you.' On the word 'Florette' Julian pouted and rolled the R way back in his throat. 'Or Manon herding the goats...'

A juicy burp sounded from above us.

'It's late. They have a right to complain. Dessert inside?' He looked at the thermometer. It was almost midnight and it was still thirty degrees. 'I have *tarte tatin* and homemade cinnamon ice cream...'

Crack. The shutters opened one more time. 'Salauds!'

Yvette clearly knew a lot of words for bastard.

As we crept out of the garden, Julian kicked aside a perfectly formed dog turd. 'Bless, O Lord, these gifts to our use and us to thy loving service,' he said, his lapsed Catholic's humour always at the ready in an emergency. 'And keep us ever mindful of the needs of others.'

The next morning at five o'clock I lay in bed, my feet thrust out of the damp sheets, listening to the sound of the radio station Chérie FM bouncing between the walls in the street below. I crept to the window, drew the curtain to one side and looked out. Yvette had placed a pink plastic radio on the kitchen sill that faced our bedroom. She had closed her own window and left the station's heroine, Celine Dion, to blurt a coded message of hatred into our sleep.

'Are you awake?' I asked Julian.

'No, I am not,' Julian snatched another snore from the hot air. 'I'm asleep. Burn some lavender or sage or something. Try and send them some loving kindness. Aren't you supposed to be the good Buddhist round here?' He turned onto his back and pulled a pillow over his head.

I tripped into the street and stood outside the door in my Winnie-the-Pooh tee shirt and knickers. The sun was just appearing behind the hills and the stone of the buildings glowed pink in its light. An olive tree puffed a cloud of twittering finches out into the warm morning air. Celine belted out I love you, please say you love me too. I belted out I hate you to the Grouillers' bottle-green shutters, and with the dawn the romance was drained from Crillon le Brave forever.

I bought my painting of lavender fields as Julian was preparing dinner on a beautiful warm June evening. Walking by his studio on our way to dinner in the village,

I glanced in and was propelled through the door. He was kind enough to let me interrupt him and the painting I chose reminds me to live in the now, and of a walk down narrow winding streets of unexpected pleasures.

Melinda Maloon, Ojai, California, USA

Two Pomegranates

I got married (at age 50!) last year to a wonderful man who loves to cook, and particularly loves garlic. When I saw 'Still life with garlic heads, knife and jar,' I knew I had to have it!

Jane Lynch, office manager, Greenville, South Carolina, USA

JULIAN PROPOSED TO ME driving at seventy miles an hour round the London orbital. Once I had figured out what he was trying to say, and had agreed, he stopped off in a Kentish town and bought us two bicycles as an engagement present to ourselves. A month later, wedding invitations were sent out depicting one pomegranate with a squished crown leaning into another with a pert one, and I was pregnant.

We had met a year before at a wedding in Devon. I was playing a Bach cello suite in a midnight blue frock, underneath which I wore leather walking boots in readiness for the hike to the ceremony. Julian, in identical boots (Zamberlan, I think they were) and a Paul Smith suit, was serving the champagne. He had heard there might be girls at the event and had spent the summer at the pool in Bedoin developing a tan and muscles. Now he was showing off the tan and the muscles beneath rolled shirtsleeves as he filled my glass between bourrées, and that was how the flirting began.

Later, on the banks of a river, a flute played in the reeds, words of love were uttered, poems were recited and Julia and Michael were wed. A child came around with a basket of wildflower seeds and ribbons, and we were asked to scatter the seeds on the ground with our wishes for the happy couple. Distracted by the handsome barman, I forgot to let mine go.

Then we were asked to tie our ribbons on the branch of a tree. Although I was supposed to be sending loving vibrations to the bride and groom, all I could think about was where the barman was going to tie his ribbon and how close I could get mine to it. I watched as he tied a sailing knot on a low branch. I noticed how his nails were cut, how the tendons moved like rivers up his forearm as he threaded one end of the red satin through the other. I fixed my eye on a place on the same branch as and a quarter of an inch away from the place from which he was now turning away.

As I contemplated the position, I remembered the bride's words about her artist friend. The man who lived in Provence. The man who had put his arms around her on a cliff face when she had been sobbing with vertigo. The man who made his own pasta, who knew the director of every film and the name of every plant and bird in the Vaucluse; who had shared a student bed with her brother, to whom the brother, Gary, was still a fiercely loyal friend. The man with twinkly blue eyes and golden curls. The man who was a promising painter. The man I would have to wait two years to meet but probably the nicest man she knew (apart, of course, from the one she had just married).

I took my ribbon and I wound it twice around the branch next to this man's. I tied a neat bow and thought: this is the man I will marry. We walked back together along the riverbank and I slipped my packet of wildflower seeds into his pocket.

After dinner there was more music and poetry. There was much more champagne. And then there was a cabaret. Toward its end the compere randomly picked two people from among the guests—Julian and me. The compere proceeded to direct us in a play about love and revenge: now you signal your distress; now you tackle her lover; now you stab the bad stepfather; now you run toward him; now you run toward her; now you...

Now, a few months after his proposal, Julian and I were about to be married. We were standing at the base of a silver birch tree whose boughs shivered with spring growth. Underneath the tree sat a string quartet and an organ, and rows of chairs fanned out from its trunk. As I walked from the herb garden to the place where we would make our home-grown vows, cream organza fluttered at my bare calves and my fingers clutched at sea lavender. A Bach chorale mingled with the bleating of sheep. Now we were saying I do. Now, in place of wedding bells, Rumi's words rang out on the June air:

I want to hold you close like a lute
so we can cry out with loving.

I looked down at the base of the tree trunk, at a pair of sculpted feet in stone-coloured Birkenstocks. This was the man I was going to spend my life with, and this tree was our church.

Go now to your dwelling
and may your days be good and long upon the earth.

Now the last lines of our ceremony were being gobbled up by a breeze as we skipped toward the farm gate and into our future together as man and wife.

'Thank you for marrying me,' I said.

'Someone had to,' said my husband.

22

I hung the Persimmon in our New York kitchen last year, finding the orange glow and its background dark just suited to our newish marriage and its own gleam and background.

Mary Ann Caws, prof. of comparative literature, New York, USA

Boats at Carry-le-Rouet

*I do live scoring for local theater, working collaboratively
during rehearsals to develop melodies, moods, and sound
effects that come directly from the actors' lines or move-
ments. My Postcard from Provence print was my gift to
my husband for our wedding.*

Kira, cellist, Austin, Texas, USA

MARRIED LIFE HAD WELL AND TRULY BEGUN and we
were sitting Mac to Mac at the kitchen table. Wires
were tangled everywhere because, perched on a hill in the
Vaucluse, we were still on dial-up. Julian glanced above my
head at a portrait on which he had been working now for
three years. He had declared it finished and the sitter had
written asking if he could make her eyes less froggy. He
winced and looked back down at his screen.

'I'm forwarding you an email I just received.'

'OK,' I said.

He passed the cable across. I connected and read the
email from a Dutch art consultant asking for a quote for five
still life paintings for the Queen Mary 2 cruise ship.

'On second thoughts,' he said, 'it's probably just someone taking the piss.'

I googled the Queen Mary.

'Wow, Julian! Listen to this! "Soaring public rooms, ten restaurants, a grand ballroom, a 360 degree promenade deck... make a grand descent down the sweeping stairway of the splendid, three-storey Britannia Restaurant, reminiscent of the opulent dining salons of the past..." '

'It doesn't mean a thing.'

'You are not going to reply?'

'The Web is seductive and you, my love, are deliciously naïve. Pass the cable over, I'm marking it as trash.'

I took the lead between my thumb and forefinger but was unwilling to go further. 'Hang on. At least give this bloke an answer!'

Julian pulled the cable from my machine. 'You don't understand, this is not from a real person. It is a computer-generated junk thing that just goes to anyone who has "still life painting" written into their HTML.'

'OK. If you're not going to reply, I'll do it.'

I wrenched the cable out of his laptop, plunged it into mine and switched over to Julian's gmail. I found the letter in the trash and clicked Reply.

'120 x 90 whatsimetres centipedes whatever. Come on! How much?'

Julian was tugging at a nasal hair and I wanted to slap him.

'Probably three or four thousand euros each...,' he said.

'Right, I'm sending them a quote.'

The response from the art consultant was immediate and positive. His company inquired about a further four landscapes to be made into prints for the first class cabins. A month later a contract was on the table.

In the weeks that followed, Julian moved like an athlete with the wind behind him from maquettes and charcoal outlines to big painty canvasses. In and out of the studio marched garlic and onions, olive oil, red wine and white wine. There were peaches, apricots, figs and melons. There was bread, a croissant, and cheese. There were pistou plates and coffee bowls, confit pots and teapots. There were backdrops made from Balinese ikats, Rajastan silk, Irish linen, mudcloth from Bamako and a sarong brought back from some forgotten beach by a friend. Even the humming sped up, with jaunty Handel bass lines and odes to joy replacing the usual sombre hymns and ballads. All the while I, and a sketch of a snowy house in Stony Brook, looked on. In the year and a half I had known him, I had never seen Julian paint like this. In fact, until now, I realized, I had rarely seen him paint at all.

'I hardly recognise him!' I said to my friend Jane. 'He gets up at seven and goes to the studio and I lie in bed and listen to him whizz that sable across the canvas, and all I can think of is dragging him back to bed and ripping those painty trousers off. You know he doesn't wear knickers underneath them?'

'That's pretty hot,' said Jane.

'Apparently it's just one item too much. When he gets up he's in such a hurry to see if his apples have misbehaved during the night, he doesn't even bother brushing his teeth. He hasn't shaved for three weeks.'

'Ouch. Too hot.'

'Except he's so involved in whether or not his plums and pears are sitting down properly that he doesn't have any space in his head for... '

From downstairs I heard the industrious clunk of the easel being lowered and a canvas being unscrewed from it.

'You know, Janie, I could get into being a kept woman.'

Fishing Boats, Cassis

*'I have downloaded some of Julian's paintings with the
town names in the titles so when I come to Provence next
year I can try to visit the same locations like the Impres-
sionists did in years past.'*

Michael Rodman, painter, San Francisco, California, USA

IT IS SUPERBOWL SUNDAY, but there is another reason it is
an historic day in San Francisco Bay. The Queen Mary 2 is
drawing into port. Michael is out there among the thousands
recording it, not on a digital camera or a mobile phone, but
in the time-honoured way of capturing a scene. On canvas.
From where he stands on Pier 27, the ship is awesome. It
looks twice the length of Alcatraz, higher than the Marin
Headlands, and is surely too tall to get under the Golden
Gate Bridge. Yet, as red helicopters buzz round its sleek body
like wasps, it ploughs nobly on. Sailboats flap in its wake like
handkerchiefs and it does not flinch. People gather on the
Golden Gate Bridge like matchsticks and there is hooting and
whistling and whooping as the liner slips into the finger pier.
Michael opens his Pochade box made from French walnut
and slides the palette across. He takes out his paints, a clean
board and, lastly, his greatest tool, his palette knife. Soon
he realizes that the marks he is going to need to capture the

ship's body are as big as those he uses for the entire length of Pacific Avenue! The funnel will need as substantial a blob as he would give for a painted lady and the lifeboats at her waistline are specks double the size of the roofs at Fisherman's Wharf. It is going to be quite a task.

The news reporter startles Michael when he approaches. He wants to know who and what inspired Michael to be here today, painting en plein air.

'*I got my inspiration to become a street painter when I first visited Paris and found Place du Tertre near Sacré Coeur. I watched the artists squeezed shoulder to shoulder, painting scenes and selling to the tourists and as I watched, I was amazed at how much art was produced and sold in the summer season alone. I thought of my own painting style and said to myself, If these guys can do this, there is room for one more painter in the world and that painter, 'c'est moi.' That was in 1995 and I have been inspired to paint, en plein air, ever since. On my return from France, I set up at the bottom of the famous crooked street, Lombard Street, and got to work. This year marks my sixth full year as an outdoor painter who lives solely on the sales of my paintings in the San Francisco Bay Area.*

I became interested in Julian Merrow-Smith's painting one day early on because painting en plein air is my favorite thing to do, other than travel to France. I signed up when he had been doing the postcards for about 3-4 months and I reviewed all the archive files looking for red dots, looking at his compositions and at what people were buying. Anyroad, I'd better get on otherwise she will be gone... '

Michael starts to paint, capturing the ship immediately,

brilliantly, in broad strokes of black, red and white. He has no idea that his hero's works may be on board.

Still Life with Summer Fruits

I N AUGUST 2003, something unhelpful happened. The temperature soared. That month, almost fifteen thousand people in France died from the heat. Many of the victims' corpses, in the capital, were kept in inflatable tents in a refrigerated storeroom at a disused farmers' market. Meanwhile politicians and Paris hospital workers enjoyed their vacation in cooler climes. In Crillon le Brave, shutters stayed shut and people stayed in because the word was out. It was a *canicule*.

Despite the energetic start to the Queen Mary commission, the incessant heat now slowed the pace to a virtual halt. During the day it rose to forty degrees, and at night it rarely dropped below twenty. It was too hot to sleep, too hot for sex and, more critically, it was far too hot to work. Julian's right shoulder was almost frozen and his vision was starting to blur.

Day after day, I watched as the fifth and final still life set-up disintegrated. The home-preserved plums made it onto the canvas just in time before an unsavoury film of pond life began to cover them. Julian managed to capture the apples before they started to collapse in the middle and seep fecund juices over the white linen cloth, but the pears— as yet unpainted—were sagging. The quince, which had exploded onto the stale bread, was attracting flies. What, on the canvas, appeared to be a pretty green reflection on the lemon rind was, in fact, mould.

'I'm never going to finish,' Julian mumbled in between agitated refrains of 'The Wee Purple Fella,' his brush slithering between his first and second fingers. 'I think I'd better just email them and say I can't do it.'

Another week passed. Nothing changed. The deadline drew closer. The temperature stayed high and the whisky bottle got low. Even the flies stopped moving.

'Will they mention your stillives.com website underneath the paintings?' I asked.

'I've got no idea. I've got no control. I couldn't give a... '

'It would be such good publicity. Imagine the... '

'Look. The paintings will never make it onto the ship. At worst they will never leave Crillon le Brave. At best I'll finish them and they'll end up on the CEO's office wall in Amsterdam. Forget about it.'

Two more weeks. Weeks in which a fan whirring at full throttle felt like hot breath on our faces. A film of sweat clamped onto our skin at night. Cats padded limply round the empty streets, Monsieur Grouiller was nowhere to be seen, or heard, and Provençal life was reduced to a silent movie viewed only through one shutterless window.

September arrived. Nothing changed. Then, one day in its second week, it cooled down. It dropped ten degrees overnight, the process of decay was halted and, in twenty-four hours, the fifth painting was finished. It was packed in Côtes du Rhône boxes plastered with fragile stickers and sent, along with the other four waiting in the hallway, on its way to the most luxurious ocean liner in the world.

Julian placed the virtual images, available, he told me proudly, in a choice of 600 x 452 or 890 x 671 pixels and each with its own drop shadow, under the category Still

Lifes on stillives.com. He gave each its title: *Still life with lemons*; *Still life with quince and preserved plums*; *Still life with oysters*; *Still life with summer fruits*; and *Petit déjeuner*. Now, all the artist wanted to do was to sit in front of the TV with a big glass of something very cold and very alcoholic and watch hot cyclists climb up mountains. Unfortunately the fridge was empty. Unfortunately the Tour de France had come and gone. Unfortunately Julian would have to wait for another summer.

THEY WEREN'T THERE!' GEORGE SAID as soon as his first foot was inside the door.

George and Christine owned a substantial quantity of Julian's works, including a mad piece he had done after visiting the Beaubourg ('Look! I've done a huge Bonnard!'), and a very tall self-portrait in our neighbour's late husband's suit called *Le Costume*. They had made the crossing over from the States to Europe on the Queen Mary 2 and were looking forward to seeing more of his work on the cruise.

'We looked everywhere. We asked everyone. No one had heard of this Merrow-Smith guy.'

I knew George to be a very sharp man. He had uncovered some spectacular dirt on an orchestra we both worked for that never paid its musicians and he had been right about some pretty crazy stuff. Surely, however, he was wrong about this?

'They were certainly not in the dining room. Britannia, did you say?'

Julian took our guests' coats and laid them over his bicycle. His movement, usually so fluid (Julian is the best dancer I know), seemed unnatural. He led George and Christine upstairs, where he removed the cork from a bottle with a shoulder-jamming pull. He filled four glasses unusually high and began to ask them about life in Santa Barbara. Had they had forest fires this year, he asked. His vowels seemed to be glued to the back of his teeth. If so, he continued, was it because of the eucalyptus? What a shame, he said. What a marvellous tree, and what a scent! What about that sweet gallery-cum-café on the main drag? Any interesting exhibitions recently? Christine gently tried to bring us back to the subject of the Queen Mary. Julian interrupted her. 'And is George still playing the horn?' he asked.

The subject of Julian's first real professional success was clearly closed. Not until Joyce came along in the comments box, four years later, was it reopened.

My husband and I knew that there were Still Lifes by Julian on the QM2 so we unpacked the minute we got on the ship, and began our quest to find them, a quest that was initially very frustrating.

We had a print of one of Julian's landscapes in our state room, but where were the Still Lifes? Days passed and many questions were asked. Niente. Nada. Nobody seemed to know. One day we had had our lunch, early as usual, and we crossed the restaurant to say hello to friends who were seated on the far left side as one descends the stairway. My husband glanced into the Annex (the Annex, I had gleaned from the maitre d', opened thirty minutes after the Britannia itself) and pointed. There they were! I pestered the maitre d', he agreed to change our seating arrangements, and we ate there at noon almost every day, at 'our' table. I was always careful to move the little vase that contained a flower that touched the painting. Quelle horreur! Maybe it was trying to GET IN the painting, à la Alice in Wonderland.

One of the most delightful discoveries was seeing the plaque that Julian had had engraved for his work. It is subtly placed on the left side as one walks out. It says:

Still Lifes
Julian Merrow-Smith
1959—
Still Lives

That I hadn't known that the plural of STILL LIFE is STILL LIFES is quite embarrassing. It is also 'awesome' (as undergraduates say these days) to know that Julian still lives

Joyce Lowrie, Prof. of French emerita, Wesleyan, Connecticut, USA

Palette Knife

I keep one of Julian's self-portraits hanging in my studio, and every time I look at it, he seems to be asking me, when are you going to paint?

Barbara Geri, artist and SAHM, Seattle, Washington, USA

THE FIRST PORTRAIT OF ME was done just after we lost the baby.

I hadn't seen Julian put on his painty trousers in many months. I loved his painty trousers—a pair of Levi's 501s so stiff with dried oil paint that they seemed to stand to attention in the corner of the room. Patient, understanding the leap of faith needed for them to be filled with flesh and bone. Some mornings I thought I saw them twitch with anticipation when the choice between outfits was being made, and sag slightly when they were yet again rejected in favour of clean jeans.

Julian put them on now. He slid his ballet feet into the legs and all the colours of Provence were stroked down his thighs as if by invisible fingers, giving him an ochre bum, a poppy coloured groin, and one olive knee. Next came the tee shirt. It was an old favourite from the days of the Renoir Cinema. In the middle of it was a criss-cross of marks where he would flick the brush before twirling it in another colour.

The last thing he had painted, as far as I could remember, was a reine claude plum, and I could see the palette now: bright green lake, cerulean blue, alizarin crimson, pthalo green, cadmium yellow deep, raw umber, ultramarine, burnt sienna, titanium white, coral orange and yellow ochre.

'How about sitting for a portrait?' he said. 'You look beautiful.'

Julian took my hand and led me up the spiral staircase and down again, into the kitchen and out, and all through the bedrooms looking for a place where the light was adequate. When we arrived at the bathroom he stopped. His head was almost touching the ceiling where it met the top of the window. We had been doing some insulation work on it, and above us a quilted space-blanket was oozing from either side of two metal bars where we had not secured the plaster-board. Around the window frame the render had been exposed after hours of my chipping at the concrete, and the rubble was in a small pile below. Under our feet the tiles were cracked. There was a smell of herbal toothpaste and Penhaligon's 'Blenheim Bouquet.' Julian placed a stool in front of the window and started sawing the legs off his easel. 'Here,' he said. 'This is where I shall paint you.'

'Isn't the ceiling a bit low?'

'The light's good.' Julian was muttering to himself about the days growing shorter as he amputated his easel, as if the days and the easel were shrinking in tandem. He changed the angle several times and then he got his paintbrushes out. 'Been a while since I've used these.'

I took off my robe and sat. Looking at Julian's face I realised that the time for compliments was over, that my nakedness was nothing to him now but shapes and shadows, and I fixed my gaze on a piece of bare knee showing through the hole in his jeans. A crust of paint on the frayed denim framed the flesh, and the skin was pale. A few hairs from the bottom of his thigh were mixed up with the threads of the torn material and were knitting together. He swished his brush back and forth, stopping only to dab at nipples of paint, squeeze the last bit of colour out of a tube or immerse a brush in white spirit, flicking it to and fro across the rim of the jar so that the wood went 'ting' on the glass. Little hummings escaped his lips, pursed in concentration, and his eyes were half closed to the world of solid things. Four red-wood stretcher bars linked together to form a square, and across that square was a canvas on the other side of which my face was apparently appearing stroke by stroke. I shivered and listened to Monsieur Grouiller droning on in the street below. The time passed slowly, achingly. I tried to focus but my eyes glazed over. Suddenly I heard the sound of ripping. I looked up to see a palette knife being thrust through the canvas. It was coming toward my face with an almost sexual violence. I ducked. Through the gash I saw Julian standing with his back toward me, looking out of the window. He had thrown his brushes on the floor and they had landed like pick-up sticks. He was cursing Mary and damning God and telling Christ Almighty that he'd made a right cock-up putting a set of brushes in his hand. He was using the c-word and the f-word and both of them in conjunction with the holy son. I moved over to him and put my hand lightly on his shoulder. 'Perhaps we should take a break?'

Julian pushed me away. 'I don't need solutions,' he said. 'I'll be all right. I'll go out for a walk and then I'll start another one. I want to do this.'

Seven hours later, after Julian had blasphemed his way up and down the road a few times and started a new painting, and as the blood-orange light of a setting sun was coming in through the window, he plunged the tips of his brushes into the murky white spirit for the last time. As their tops relaxed outward on the base of the yoghurt pot, he turned the easel round. I looked, aghast. 'Wow,' I said. On the canvas was a face ravaged by grief, its mouth an open wound. 'You got me there.'

'Yes, I think I did. Not quite what I thought would come out, but then again it never is.'

I pulled a towel from where it was draped over the shower cubicle, and wrapped it around my body.

'You looked sad,' said Julian, 'and I had to paint that even though I wanted to paint you all released and gorgeous. Sorry.'

Portrait of a Woman

I have done quite a lot of sitting in my life. When I was a girl I sat for my aunt, a very good watercolour painter, who taught me how to sit and be still. At a strange phase of my life, when I needed the money, I was a life model for a while, with a little electric fire to keep me warm. You could have bought a study of me from a shop in Leominster. And now, in my calm maturity (just kidding), I was sitting for a portrait by Julian.

Sitting for Julian tends to be either quite or extremely amusing. The experience ranged from listening to a whole hour of the Archers to hearing entire Mozart or Rameau operas. A rather nervous Julian at the start of painting would hum all the most beautiful soprano arias in a key perhaps not quite suited to his voice. I speak as a singing teacher.

We talked a great deal, the conversations were always interesting or great fun, or the other way round. We discussed film, of which Julian knows a lot after managing an art cinema in one of his previous lives. Of course we never gossiped about the people we knew. Occasionally Julian took photographs; mainly he stood over there staring at me. At times I found it hard not to giggle, which must be why the picture has been described as having the quizzical look of the Mona Lisa. Julian keeps a mirror in

*his studio, and would check the image in the mirror. This
was to make sure I was the right way up.*

*As an afternoon progressed, Julian's white tee shirt
grew more and more splattered with paint. Now I know
why so many tee shirts are sold in the world. Sometimes I
gazed at him thoughtfully. I was trying to count how many
brushes he could hold in his hand at one time.*

*For all the amusement, the experience is demand-
ing and intense, the intensity arises out of the long close
serious scrutiny of your face by the other person. Time
and sessions passed. We would pause to drink tea out of
beautiful David Garland cups. Sometimes we heard the
heavenly sound of a cello playing in another room.*

Mo Duckworth, singer, Ledbury, UK

MY PORTRAIT was leaning against the skirting board
on the fourth step of the Victorian terraced house. I
presumed it was still trying to decide whether it would live
alone in Peckham with my father, to whom we had given
it at Christmas, or with his wife in the Oxford home they
occasionally shared.

'What do you think about when you see it now?' I asked
Julian.

'I think that it was bloody freezing,' said Julian, 'that
I had to cut the legs off my easel because the ceiling was so
low, and that I was painting in a bathroom. I had scrambled
eggs for breakfast. I remember that this head was cut down
from a large nude I never really finished. What do you see?'

Tom called down the stairs, his melodic voice, as usual,
sounding like lines from an avant-garde opera. 'Be with you
in a sec. Just finishing off.'

'I see a woman with goose-bumps who is pissed off

about posing naked in February...'

I knew some of our friends were uncomfortable with the portrait, perhaps because a painting, like music, can speak the unspeakable. Then again, the unspeakable can render us more translucent. I looked harder at the woman. Her right shoulder jutted forward. A blurred right eye was looking back into the canvas while the left appeared to be marching into her childless future. A lock of hair had broken free from her comb and formed a question mark, which was answered by the tip of the pony tail curling around her neck, leading the way across her collarbone, out of the picture, between her breasts, over her stomach and down to the scar which I knew travelled from hip to hip. I had put on almost twenty pounds since then. Silver hairs were beginning to sprout from my temples, and two deep lines jostled for importance where the slope of my nose used to turn seamlessly into my forehead.

'It wasn't February, it was October,' said Julian.

'Come up,' called my father.

When we entered the kitchen, Tom was hunched, as he seemed to have been all my life, over a table, and was clipping at pieces of hair. His aging left hand didn't seem to have left his silver jubilee mug of milky tea in thirty-five years, except perhaps to pinch the filter off a gauloise. On the edge of the table was a keyboard of cigarette burns.

'It's good, isn't it?' I said. 'The portrait. Do you like it?'

Tom had never praised Julian as an artist, probably because praise was not something he himself sought or needed, and Julian had never expected praise from someone in whose league he would never aspire to be.

'It's the best thing he's ever done,' said Tom, looking briefly up and over his tartan spectacles. 'As I've said in my book about good portraiture, if you turned it to the wall I would feel like someone had just left the room. Portraiture is a funny thing. I try and explain the process to my sitters by saying that it simply involves two people in a room, one of whom is trying to be painted by the other.'

Tom laid down his tools, brushed them to one side of the table and took off his glasses.

'By the way, there's a bottle of—well, you'll recognise it—let's drink that together. No fun drinking it on my own and Fiona doesn't drink, except for champagne, as you know.'

I looked at the random display on the wall: a series of orange peels cut, fashioned into pitted penises and framed, a ravishing charcoal fantasy of a musical score and an invitation to some event involving the Queen at which I supposed my father would wear the same blue Nikes as he wore to her garden party. Julian busied himself with opening the bottle of 1999 Chateau Rayas.

'Have you got any interesting commissions?' I asked.

'Oh—' the syllable fell into Tom's beard and joined what, I suspected, remained of the tinned sardines he had had on toast for lunch, '—this and that. You know. I'm making a sudoku puzzle from the autumn leaves I gathered in Princeton. These beard collages. And I am writing the text for an exhibition of two thousand postcards called We Are The People. There's a book on gold-weights to do next, a marble panel for Westminster Cathedral, working on a chamber opera of the Heart of Darkness with Tarik... Pretty busy, I'd say.'

There was a brief silence in which I could hear reggae music from the house opposite, the cricket commentary from upstairs and a child crying. Then Tom said: 'My neighbours opposite. They adopted a baby from China. Such a... They are so happy. Are you... ?'

'We're fine, dad.'

'If it's a question of money, you know I'd always help you out... '

'Thank you. Really. Honestly, we're fine. We have a wonderful life.'

Julian's portrait of my dearest daughter is full of love especially since it shows its love in acceptance of the real rather than projection of an ideal. Painting one's nearest and dearest is the tenderest subject and the hardest task.

Tom Phillips, RA, painter, Peckham, London, UK

Still Life with Autumn Fruits

A DAM'S EMAILS ON THE SUBJECT of his large commission were sent from his BlackBerry and they were to the point. He was clearly a man who knew what he wanted: He wanted a painting that would fit exactly on his dining room wall. He wanted something that had a 'kitchen flavour.' He suggested a range of vegetables, fruit, pans, bottles, cups, bread, and utensils. Julian sent him the images of the Queen Mary paintings. Adam replied by return that he wanted the pickled fruit in Still life with summer fruits, the bread basket in Still life with oysters and 'maybe a half-cut loaf of bread on a chopping board.' He wanted a fairly neutral backdrop in an earthy type of colour (maybe a sandstone wall?). He also wanted the painting with shadows, etc, in a style similar to that of a painting by Julian of a single iris that he already owned and opposite which he planned to hang the still life. He asked Julian how long it would take and Julian replied that each of the QM2 paintings had taken about three weeks, that he already had a commission of irises for his solicitor outstanding, and that he would therefore expect to finish Adam's commission in one to three months. A deposit would be required, with completion date for 15th June. Just before Julian signed off, he made the mistake: 'And I will show you stages as I get to them,' he wrote. 'How's that?'

Adam transferred the deposit immediately. Julian made

a swift start, a meditative painting of a single apple, bread, two walnuts, cheese, a knife, two preserve jars and a bowl of apples. These were given a stone-coloured background that brought a sense of the outside in and gave the objects space to breathe. Meanwhile, in the right third of the painting, a shard of light fell upon the cheese and the apple. The light energized the apple so much it seemed to be spinning. And yet it sat so quietly. Although, in the bottom left corner, one apple in the bowl and a napkin remained unfinished, Julian was excited. He thought it one of the best paintings he had done. He wrote to Adam. 'Adam, not quite finished but here is the painting set-up. I have taken a few liberties as far as contents go. Let me know what you think.'

Adam wrote back by return. In fact he wrote back so fast Julian wondered if he had even had time to open the image and view the painting. The email was seven lines long and consisted of a bullet list of four points. The first informed Julian that the cheese, knife, jars and bread were excellent. The second informed him that the overall effect was sombre and that it might be beneficial to introduce some colour as in oranges, lemons or limes. The third asked him to introduce the pot, bottle and aubergine from *Summer fruits*, and the fourth asked for a stone wall with visible mortar joints.

Julian walked over to the bag-in-box and applied some pressure with his thumb. He tilted the container slightly and the liquid whooshed into his beaker. Then he sat down at the computer to fashion a reply. Three hours later he sent this:

Hi Adam

Thanks for your response. I must say I am very pleased with the result so far and only wish that all the QM2 paintings had been this good. Looking at these things on the Web is, of course, not ideal but I include a copy with slightly more realistic colour as the other had rather a blue (daylight) shift.

Just to take up your points; I am sure you realise it takes a long time to get a set-up that's balanced, and that this is as important a part of the process as the painting and takes some days. Originally the plum jar was a bottle but it was too dominating and I changed it, but that was during the preliminary phase (underpainting, etc) and I wouldn't want to change/add anything now. The fruit bowl is just sketched in and in it are/will be apples, as I want to continue the splashes of dark red and light green that run through the painting from the apple and jars to the bowl. The light just catches a couple of the apples and will bring a little light to that corner. The overall feeling is of stillness and, critically, a particular sense of light/lightfall. I feel it is also very important to have areas of focus like the cheese, apple and walnuts in the foreground. All the triangles and convergent lines in the composition draw you to this point which is placed on the golden section. Hence the shadowy nature of the left side. The danger is to have too much going on and you end up with what I call the wallpaper effect. I cannot really add the stone look background, I can tone down or ignore things that are there but would find it difficult to add things that are not. Julian

Julian pressed Send. Then he turned the box of wine on its head and squeezed the last drops from it. When he sat back at the computer, Adam's reply, another seven liner, was already winking in his inbox. Adam liked the change from the day-light shift, he said, and agreed about the wallpaper effect. He added two bullet points. The first asked if the sketched fruit bowl would develop further and the second enquired as to what was in the bottom left corner of the painting. Julian set about typing his reply.

Hi Adam, thanks for your response. The unfinished areas are really the whole left quarter of the painting; the white cloth bottom left, the bowl and contents, and the area including the left part of the loaf around the bowl. This includes the background from the jar of pears leftward. Yes, the apples in the bowl will be very critical both in tone and colour. They are presently barely sketched in. The cloth was a late change which again is just sketched in. I felt that I needed something to stop the contents of the painting spilling out leftward and break the horizontal surface. You could say it is a kind of container which prevents the viewer's eye from wandering, forcing the eye back up through the bowl, the fruit and jars back to the wedge of cheese. The apple on the right works in a similar way. It will be finished when you get back and hopefully another one will be finished or at least, well on the way toward being finished. The format is very interesting. The other thing, of course, is scale. I had a look at it again and the size really gives it something which does not come across in a photo. Julian

Julian clicked his mouse on the word 'send' inside the white oval. He wrenched Adam's canvas off the easel and pushed it paint-side against the wall. He unwrapped a blank canvas the same size from its cellophane, wiped the set-up surface clean with a single gesture, and crowded it instead with everything he could find in the fridge. Lemons, limes, oranges, and bell peppers. Then he shoved one of my old crimson blouses behind it and started work. Within forty-eight hours he produced a very bright, very cluttered painting that he abhorred. That he also turned paint-side against the wall.

I had been to the Vaucluse with my wife many times, and we were always wandering in and out of galleries. Once we walked into a gallery where there was an English painter and I liked his work. I never took his name, I never remembered the town. I tried to find him on Google when I got back but I found Julian instead. I simply typed in 'English Artist Living In Provence' and up popped stillives. com. And so I immediately commissioned a painting. The low point of the commission was when I received an image of a lovely painting with bread and cheese and an apple from Julian with a message that there was a bit more work to do on the apple, followed by a message a few weeks later saying he had started again. He had said it might take three months. It took twenty-six. The high point of course was the day I opened the parcel with this painting inside. It sits above an antique church pew in the kitchen of our 1920s Arts and Crafts House, Friars Cottage in Esher, Surrey, England. On the opposite wall and facing it is 'Iris'. A couple of years ago I recall Isabel staring at 'Still life with autumn fruits'. She turned to me and asked, 'Daddy—did you paint that?' I wish, I thought.

Adam Glover, chartered surveyor, Esher, Surrey, UK

Two Red Pears and an Apple

About ten years ago I began collecting pear art. First, I found a candelabra with pears, then I traveled to Provence and purchased a wooden carved apple and pear. Then I encountered the work of a local Phoenix artist, Ruth Knowles, who was in her 'pear period' and fell in love with her work. Later, I met Augustin Vargis here in Phoenix. He is originally from South America but now lives here. He has an architectural background as well as fine arts and draws the most beautiful pears. So my collection is a combination of art and objects. One of these days I'll be successful in obtaining one of Julian's pears too!

Karen Wirrig, interior designer, Phoenix, Arizona, USA

JULIAN LOOKED AROUND AT THE UNFINISHED, overdue work: Adam's apple, Hank's house, four portraits of Bonnie's grandchildren from photographs now three years old and stained with olive oil, the iris bartered for his solicitor's fee back in Sussex. The vines outside the studio turned and then fell. The paintings did not advance. Julian moved from wine to whisky macs, then on to neat whisky and wine. He drafted emails to his commissioners admitting defeat: 'Dear ... , I have been unable to finish your artwork. I have been busy falling in love, getting married, painting for Queen

Mary, trying to keep warm. My wife is away on tour and I have been living off *pommes dauphinoises*. Perhaps you would like me, at this point, to return your deposit?' Though he never sent these emails, he would occasionally receive a gentle prompt: 'Any news? Would you like more of a down payment? An up-to-date photograph?' 'More payment,' said Julian. 'Yes, that would be good.' 'Relax,' they said. 'Take your time.'

That winter Julian would rather have been doing nothing than painting raspberries next to baguettes in November, children so young their faces hadn't even formed, and imagining daisy rings behind blizzards. So he did just that. Nothing. That winter, as I toured England playing Handel, Julian fell into a depression as deep as the Long Island snow.

It was December by the time I returned from my tour. I was inspired, tired and glad to be home. Having fought for elbow room in various opera pits, having been confined to cars and tied to a rigid schedule, one-ring cookery and hand washing, I was longing to fill an entire house and spill over into the surrounding countryside. I wanted to cook soups and make winter salads, to hang sheets on a line and watch them billow across a terrace. I was desperate, also, to share with my beloved the kaleidoscope of my experiences. To talk with him about everything from how playing Handel had been like sitting in prayer every night to gossipy orchestra politics. Julian however, was used to silence, autonomy and space.

'That's a nice bit of Trout quintet you are humming, darling,' I said.

'It's not a trout, it's a bossa nova,' said Julian, and fell back into silence.

I tried again. 'That guy in Hampshire's kids? That's going to be lovely...'

'I gave up on that ages ago. Please don't talk about it.'

'How's Adam's app—?'

'Please, Ruthie. Don't push me. You are always pushing me. I don't want to talk about it.'

I changed tack. 'I know what you mean, by the way, about the container you were talking about to Adam. It's like those squares of slate we had instead of plates in the restaurant the other day. I was terrified that my purée was going to run away...'

More silence.

Chantecler

*This little painting will be hung in my tiny North Carolina
mountain cabin. The cabin was once an apple shed at the
edge of an orchard, and when someone turned it into a
home, the place was named Apple Tree Cottage for the
150 year old remnant tree that grew in front of it. Sadly,
we had to have the tree cut just last summer, but we'll
hang the painting in honor of that huge tree-that-was.*

Helen Correll, Spartanburg, South Carolina, USA

JULIAN AND I HAD BEEN TIPTOEING around each other for
a week when I snuck into the studio one morning. The
vine at the window had been cut away and in the unforgiv-
ing light I saw a thick layer of dust under which stacks of
canvases seemed to be frozen in time. I pulled several paintings away from the wall, breaking up cobwebs as I did so.
Four blonde heads, a large area with the sketchy outline of
a house underneath an orange wash, some onions. Then I
found what I was looking for. There were the plums that I
loved. There was the knife and the bread and there, in the
bottom left hand corner, was the unfinished apple. It was
then that I decided that I was going to find the exact apple
that was needed to finish Adam's ex still life.

'Do you have any 'Juliette' apples?' I said when I arrived

52

at the vegetable market. 'They were organic I think.'

'No, I'm afraid they are already out of season. But you should try the Reinette Clochard. Or the Chantecler. They are used traditionally for making *tarte tat—*'

I removed a crumpled visiting card from my wallet with a bad reproduction of one of Julian's apple paintings on it and showed it to Madame Sarl. The apples were not to eat, I explained, but for a still life. They had to be streaky green with red bits... I looked over to where the shop owner was pointing. A box of yellowish apples looked back at me that I found hard to imagine as the finishing touch to Adam's painting, let alone the gooey basis to Julian's favourite dessert. Their skin was dull, covered in brown freckles, and the flesh, I imagined, would be mealy.

'You should try English apples!' I said to the owner.

'I went to England once,' she replied. 'The food was terrible. Listen, I can see you are unsure. I'll give you two as a gift.' She placed two of the matte apples in my hand. 'One for you and one for your painter friend.'

In the privacy of the car I took a bite. Despite its dowdy skin, the apple was crisp and sweet. It made me think of tree houses, bramble bushes after rain, wellington boots and crumble. When I got home with Julian's Chantecler I realized I was so excited by the new taste I had forgotten Adam entirely.

'That's no good,' said Julian. 'You know I only like small flat apples, and if they are yellow... well, they just can't be yellow. They have to be gold with some kind of blush on them...'

'Just taste it,' I said. 'By the way, I forgot to tell you...'

'And they have to sit!'

' ... last week there was a label on one of the *Marchés de Provence* boxes that read Pink Kiss. I explained to the them politely that the apple's name translated as *Bisou Rose*.'

Julian took a bite. 'Christ, where did you get these?'

'This week they had a new sign up saying 'Pink Kiss' and underneath it was written: *'Bisu Rose'* but mis-spelled, which was charming...'

'Mmm...'

'...but above the Braeburns there was now a sign that read Bred—'

'They are delicious!'

'Of course the woman in the shop, the only French-woman I have ever seen with crocs, had to slag off every single variety of English apple though I'm sure she's never—'

'Listen to me, Ruthie!'

'And she gave me this, so I gave her the stillives web address so she could go and see her vegetables on the Queen Mary...'

'It's like a Russet and Worcester Pearmain...'

'You like it?' I asked, listening at last. I may not have found Adam's apple, I thought, but I had, apparently, found a good French *pomme*.

'It's like a Russet and Worcester Pearmain and a Cox's Orange Pippin all rolled into one. I'm exaggerating of course.'

'Which you never do.'

'But...,' Julian took another bite. 'Oh, darling, it's good to have you home!'

Mont Ventoux from Les Couguieux

*During the ascent of the Mont Ventoux I imagined Julian
sitting somewhere in the fields, painting. Maybe I was tired
of all the cycling and my brain was functioning in a strange
way but sometimes it felt like we weren't cycling the Mont
Ventoux region, we were cycling Julian's landscapes.*

Luc Shuddnick, hospital pharmacy assistant, Schellebelle, Belgium

OUR FIRST VISIT TO THE HOUSE AT LES COUGUIEUX was
in autumn. The cyclists had taken their taut bodies
back to their office jobs in Frankfurt and Boston, the nudists
had put their suits and salwars back on, and the countryside had brought out its prize hues. Julian rolled down the
windows, revved up the Citroen Visa, put the hardened ball
of his bare foot on the gas pedal and, humming the most
hummed hum in his humming repertoire, the scarecrow song
from The Wizard of Oz, sailed us down the hill in neutral.
I could wile away the hours conferrin' with the flowers. As
usual, he hummed and I imagined the words. *I would not
be just a nuffin', my head all full of stuffin'*, my heart all
full of pain. After the village of Bedoin and on the way up
toward the mountain he turned left onto a track flanked by
vineyards. The grape-picking season was ending and and we
saw Spanish and Polish workers on both sides of the road.

55

Some dozed in the sugary air, their hats tipped over their brows. Others had set up picnic tables next to the tinny red trucks that bulged with fruit, and were breaking baguettes. We coiled through cherry orchards, almond and olive groves. *I would dance and be merry. Life would be a ding-a-derry, if I only had a brain.* And arrived at a ruined hamlet. Julian pulled over.

'Oh, I know this one!' he said. 'I painted that wheat-field last year!'

We climbed out and drank in the view. Lines of crimson vines swirled out like a pleated skirt from where we stood on chocolate ploughed earth. To the right a cherry orchard seemed to have been dipped in beetroot juice and there was a custard-coloured lake of wheat to the left. The scene was punctuated in the middle distance by a butternut squash tinted field and three trees in quince green. The slopes of the Mont Ventoux rose up behind, a turban of pink clouds wound around its peak. The view that had been but a thumb-nail image in our bathroom window was now in full screen mode. No need for Neon Glow, Smudgestick, Mezzotint or Lensflare. It was all there. We turned our backs to the mountain and in front of us stood an ochre oblong with two doors and four windows outlined in peeling white. The house was attached to a crumbling ruin and a crack ran down its façade like a tear.

'*Allo!*' The shutters of the house opposite opened and a heart-shaped face beamed at the window. 'My name is Nadine. Enchanted! Will we be neighbours?'

We talked a little, establishing the facts that her partner was a sculptor and Julian a painter, and that the rest of the hamlet was likely to stay in ruins because the owner had hardly touched it in years and wouldn't sell.

'But if you move here,' she concluded, giving us a

panoramic grin, 'it will be the Artists' Hamlet and we would be *ravis!*'

We drove unusually slowly back to Crillon le Brave that day. Something had changed. In that one view of the Mont Ventoux, my resistance to leaving our rented house had melted. The silence of the hamlet had amplified the Grouillers' antics in the village, and Julian and I agreed that night that perhaps it was time to move on.

The next day I rang the estate agent only to be told that the house had been mysteriously taken off the market.

Two months later I re-emerged from another long tour. The ends of my fingers were splayed and taut as drum-skins. I had travelled hundreds of miles, playing twenty-five performances each of Carmen, Theodora and a new opera about aeroplanes in plush opera houses, shabby seaside theatres and shopping centres. I had planted my Camper soles on pit-floors of wood, sweet-wrapper covered linoleum, moth-eaten carpet and slate. I had stayed with friends in the posh-est part of London, in the most rundown part of Manchester, on a moor, above a fish and chip shop and next door to a pub. I had read three books, done fifty yoga sun salutes, and eaten far too many chana dals. Meanwhile, Julian had not left the house. His face, having hardly moved to speak for a month, was set, and his body bloated from too much wine and potatoes. It was a difficult meeting. However, there was good news. Very good news. The house at Les Couguieux had reappeared in the estate agent's window.

'Think of the cloudscapes...'

'But you saw those slabs of concrete. What is the guy who owns the ruin going to do?'

'And that crack the width of a bloody five lane highway.'

'And the length of the Mississipi.'

'Nadine said Croulard comes round once every three years, makes some noise about all the holiday homes he is going to build and then bogs off again.'

'At least then it would be quiet.'

'What's the worst-case scenario?'

'We would live in a tourist complex with faux lavender doors...'

'... swarming with sunburned English people in Marks and Spencer swimwear.'

'Buying my paintings?'

'Or Dutch.'

'No, they're too tight.'

'Or we would leave one bonkers neighbour only to move in next to another.'

'All pretty crap scenarios.'

'Yes. But that view...'

'Yes, that view.'

'And the Artists' Hamlet...'

'Sometimes it already feels like home.'

'Yes.'

'The Gallery...?'

'But it's just too dangerous, isn't it?'

'Yes.'

'I've booked an appointment with the estate agent next week.'

Moonrise over the Mont Ventoux

Like Julian, I live in a house that faces a mountain, and at the foot of a mountain that faces a house. My post-card painting is of a blue mountain, not unlike our own, Mount Monadnock. The scene has a stretch of wheat in front, lush, like summer can be here or perhaps anywhere in the world. I set the little painting on the windowsill in my kitchen, facing the mountain, facing the sun.

Edie Clark, writer, Harrisville, New Hampshire, USA

NAMED, APPARENTLY, AFTER THE STRIPEY mallow flower that lines the banks in spring, the hamlet of Les Couguieux would, at one time, have consisted of four or five farm dwellings, with its own well and caves. Now, with the exception of Nadine's house and the house we were viewing, it had fallen into the hands of Monsieur Croulard, and into disrepair. Before showing us the inside, the estate agent gave us a tour of the ruin and filled us in on some of the history. While she spoke, I could see Julian looking sadly upon the honey- and rose-coloured stones crumbling from window, well and arch back into the sandy rock face.

'The big pebbles,' said the estate agent, 'are called *galets* and they would have been gathered in the fields. You can see that each one has its own personality.'

We looked more closely. Indeed, some were dappled and flat, others rounded and speckled. They were shaped like tibia, planets, lungs and …

'… and something else,' said Julian. 'Something wonderful, I just can't remember, it's on the tip of my tongue. It is something delicious, I know.'

How bland the modern wall was in comparison, we agreed, like a row of false teeth. As we walked round the ruin, we observed lintels collapsing and a spiral staircase disintegrating. In a plaster fireplace a thrust of wild grasses grew round a cement mixer, and the overgrown courtyard was home only to a broken tractor. Where the structure was weak, someone had parked slabs of concrete on the roof. No wonder it was falling down. Hadn't the owner heard that in masonry you start with the foundation? With the first stone? When the agent led us back to the house the mood was sombre.

The house faced south and, as was customary to protect the inhabitants from the mistral, there were no windows at all in the north wall. Not ideal light for an artist, she agreed, but skylights might be a possibility 'since the building was not within view of the church.' Julian and I looked at each other, imagining priests climbing up the church spire with binoculars to peer at our love-making. The agent turned a mammoth key in the door and we entered, blinking in the darkness. When she clipped back the shutters we saw a room laid with cement tiles stained the colour of urine. Soot and dust caked every available surface, and spiders' webs were strung across the ceiling from the black beams like a tent. Clearly no one had let a summer in to warm the home for many years. We stooped to follow her through a door into a windowless hovel that was described as the kitchen. An iron pot stood on a seventies fireplace and along the cracked

walls ran wires protected only by yellowing paper. The dirt
floor was covered in animal droppings and the ceiling was
head height. So far the interior couldn't have been further
from our dream of sun-splashed terracotta. The wall would
have to go, of course, to let in some light, but would it
be enough? The only sound as the three of us climbed the
enclosed stairwell toward the bedrooms was the kicking of
rotten magazines and the crushing of soda cans underfoot.

'Be patient' said the agent, sensing the gloom. 'You
haven't seen the best bit.'

The bedrooms were in no better shape but we could see,
when we prized open the shutters, that at least the work
needed here was cosmetic. Each one housed at least four
rusty beds, their springs sagging under the weight of straw
mattresses damp with the memory of long gone sleepers.
The rooms all looked out on to a wall 'renovated' in pink
concrete. All, that was, except for the third room.

'Julian!' I cried from the doorway.

Julian did not budge. I walked back down the hall and
looked in on him. He was pacing the length and breadth
of the second bedroom with foot-long strides, and I could
tell from his eyes flickering in concentration that he was re-
vamping it in his mind, pulling down walls, moving doors
and adding curvy en-suites. Then he stood still. I imagined
what he might be thinking. A bit of caseine and wax tinted
with noir fumé and terre verte for the doors, perhaps? Or
should it be warmer, with umbers and burnt sienna? The
walls could be two colours, of course, with a line dividing
them four feet high, about here? This was something he did
in every house we visited when he thought the hosts weren't
looking and it usually made him frown. This time, however,
he was smiling. I touched him in the small of his back, led
him along the hallway to the third bedroom and opened the

door wide. In front of us a square of burnished vines was visible through an east-facing opening. Like a designer setting eyes on a swatch of material and having his Autumn Collection revealed to him, I think it was in that instant that Julian saw the potential. I looked at him standing in the middle of the room on floor tiles bleached amber and pink. The sun had turned the corner and was streaming in now through a south-facing window, illuminating his golden curls from behind. Summer freckles were scattered over his skin like confetti and the down on his forearms stood up slightly.

'I could paint here!' he said.

'There's more,' said the estate agent, leading us toward the north wall in which was set a waist-high door.

Bowing our heads, we followed her, stepping down into a space we had not even suspected to be part of the house.

'This,' she said, 'would have been the hayloft.'

Flooded with light and with a direct view of the mountain through three enormous windows, with a cathedral-height beamed ceiling and unplastered walls, Julian stood in seventy-five square metres of the kind of French barn he had always dreamed of. It was a glorious master bedroom, a luxury apartment for friends, a holiday home for when the going got tough, a concert hall...

'My studio!' he said, 'and,' he added, looking through a hole in the plaster floor to the space below, 'my gallery! Mallow Gallery. Does that sound good? Yes, I could definitely paint here.'

'If we do ever come to live in the Artists' Hamlet,' I whispered, 'and I think we just might, I promise not to mess up with the new neighbours.'

'Potatoes!' said Julian, gawping at the beauty of the masonry like Hansel at walls fashioned from candy. 'The stones are like potatoes!'

Red and Gold

How I met Julian was simple. I met him as an artist meets other artists. While surfing, doing my daily blog surveillance, I saw on the Philadelphia based webcomics artist, Charley Parker's site an article about 'Postcards from Provence' and I thought, yet another one that lives in the Luberon or in the Alpilles, but these intricate paintings pushed me to see more. I went on Julian's website. I was curious to know where the guy lived, so I saw Crillon le Brave and thought, wow, he lives so near. Be brave! Write to him! And he answers!.....

Anders Lazaret, illustrator, Les Baux, Vaucluse, France

ANDERS LAZARET'S REAL NAME is Guillame Chauvet. He has long hair that does that frizzy thing that men's hair does past a certain length, an aquiline nose and thick spectacles that frame slanted eyes. His glasses hide his good looks and turn him into the kind of gothic hero he creates on his blog, where he describes himself as the messiest guy on earth and a full-time loser. There his drawings are entitled Flattening of Emotions and The Beautiful Wound, and comments on them range from *Tu aimes la Bad Chicken Attitude* to *Ouai Sublime.* He lives with his father. He doesn't have much to say to his family because he doesn't like wine and they don't seem very interested in Edgar Allan Poe. There aren't many arty people round here and I suspect girls don't interest him much. However, he does have one passion. He loves the *Géant de Provence*: the Mont Ventoux.

At first, when he pays a visit, Anders does not talk. He arrives at the agreed-upon time, takes off his heavy boots and stands very still in his socks in the middle of the kitchen. Listening, waiting. He brings with him a silence that I am unwilling to break. Thankfully, in the end, he breaks it himself and for half an hour he cannot stop talking about the mountain.

'The giant watching over us here,' he says, his English perfect in a cyber kind of way 'I know her well, not every corner but her south side. She's quiet, beautiful. The nature is all around playing every day its play. I can't stop gazing at her. Listening, breathing, feeling alive.'

I ask him if he would like to sit. He refuses. I sit anyway. I am aware that he is very tall.

'A simple walk in the forest and worries disappear for a while, and if you're silent and respectful enough, Nature will let you see her children. A singing bird, a fox crossing the road at night, eagles flying silently, all those little marvels that make you feel better.'

Anders takes his glasses off for a moment to think and trains a stray lock of hair back over his ear. His fingers are so caring in the act I can't help but imagine the girls from the surrounding villages hiding in broom bushes waiting to catch a glimpse of this mysterious young man.

'I do a lot of rock climbing and every place offers a different view of the Mont Ventoux. From *Les Dentelles de Montmirail* you have a side view. From Venasque a facing view. From St-Léger a back view, and every time the same idea comes into your mind: wow. We're really nothing. It teaches humility and respect to those who are able and open-minded enough to listen.'

I sit and drink wine. Anders remains standing, drinking nothing, his arms long and loose by his side. I am finding it difficult to believe that this exquisite lover of nature is the author of Punish my Heaven.

'I think that for someone who comes here for the first time, the most impressive thing must be the omnipresence of colours. It's like taking a huge cup of colours and lights, filling your eyes in a second, and marking your mind forever. Anyway, I thought I was really aware, then I discovered an awesome painter! Aha! But Julian gives you the real essence in the way a photo cannot. His paintings are pieces from here, a narrative in a way. I'm sure that if he showed a rough painting with only colour on it to someone from here, as a kind of Rorschach test, the person would say: It's here!'

At his request, I hand Anders a glass of water. He takes a gulp and sets the glass almost tenderly on the table.

'Going back to the mountain... ,' he says. His eyes squint behind his glasses and for the first time I get a hint of the creator of haunting imagery. 'There is a special magic on the summit. The lunar mood of it. It's a strange sensation. It feels like you are able to fly, like you are untouchable.'

Julian has left the room. Anders is whispering now.

'By the way, I was sure that, in a worry of perfection, Julian would have this great typical southern French accent. But no, he doesn't! Aha! It is very English! See you again, I hope, dear neighbours!'

And with that, Anders leaves.

Poppy Bank

WE WERE STILL UNDECIDED about Les Couguieux. We had no doubt about the house, but we were at once daunted by the ruin and challenged to take it on. We went to see other properties. There were enticing pools and nearby rivers, pretty kitchens, gardens and roof terraces, but we returned feeling empty. After the viewings we always got drunk. Were we lovesick? We put in an offer on a house near the Toulourenc valley near our friends Jo and George. It was refused. We were relieved. We waited. We weren't sure for what.

One day in April I'd had enough. I rose and pedaled off, determined to talk to Nadine and feel out the Couguieux hamlet once and for all.

It was still early so I parked my bike against the wall and sat for a moment at the edge of the vineyard. I listened to the contented chatter of warblers and the hammer of chiffchaffs announcing the coming heat. In the distance, two cherry trees dusted with pale pink blossom formed an arch of petals, and through it the acid green shoots of the vines glimmered in the sun and lit the way to the mountain. Spring bugs hummed in the air and single poppies dotted the bank on which I sat. Gradually, as I immersed myself more and more in the presence of the Ventoux, I began to feel not only protected, but also guided by it. After a while

I was awakened from my reverie by the whirr of a cyclist's wheels. I waggled my toes and looked at my watch. The time was nine-thirty and I had been sitting there for over an hour.

I approached the neighbours' door, thinking of a few practical questions I might ask and, as I did so, I noticed a dark-skinned man in the adjoining building. He was holding something at a right angle to his body, its tip alight like a wand. His head, topped with a brightly coloured fez, was cocked in concentration toward his left shoulder and I could hear something fizzing. Below the medicinal smell of the rosemary in flower, I thought I could detect a whiff of molten wax.

'Welcome to the Foundry,' said Manuel coming out to greet me. 'Enter!'

Standing among the sensuous forms of his bronzes, I received answers to none of my questions about telephone lines, council tax or septic tanks. Indeed, though I may have been well advised to, I never asked them. Instead I followed Manuel into what he described as the best reason to buy a house at Les Cougieux: the surrounding countryside. He led me past red sand caves carpeted with thyme that, he explained, used to house troglodytes. Then into a glade of oak scrub where ribbons of light were entwined around lichen, where our feet padded on moss. It was there that he pointed out the sculpture garden he had created. Every day, he said, he laid a stone. I looked at the pieces: long *galets* placed one on top of the other to form airy cairns, and flat ones in concentric circles disappearing under mallow; a round stone in a hollow and a triangular one perched on a bough. For artists, Manuel said, Les Cougieux was a magic place, and it had a history of people who loved the mountain.

'Monsieur Archinard,' he said, 'who lived in your house once. Now there was a man who loved the Ventoux. He practically worshipped it. You ask the baker, the butcher or anyone who knew him, and whether they are rich or poor, fat or thin, they will beam at his name. He would be up at the top to watch the sun rise, or he would lead friends on moonlit vigils at night. Every day of his life, even when he was eighty-nine, he walked on it. He knew every oak tree and cedar, every lark, boar and orchid. He is buried here, in the cemetery, and unlike the fashion for extravagant porcelain baskets of fruit and angels, Archinard simply has a stone from his beloved mountain on his grave. That is the kind of man he was.'

As I was leaving I said, 'Maybe one day we will be neighbours?'

'I would like that,' said Manuel.

I smiled and shook his hand. 'Me too.'

I returned to Crillon to deliver my final verdict to Julian:

'With the Mont Ventoux behind us, a history of troglothingies, boars running wild, a pair of snogging cherry trees, a stone sculptor next door, exquisite whiffs everywhere, and the toilet for once in my life—and yours I think—not in the prosperity corner, we could be in for some seriously good feng shui. We'll just have to take a chance on the ruin.'

...And the big surprise was that this artist lives nearer than I thought. Not in the Alpilles. Not even in Crillon le Brave. Julian and Ruth are neighbours of an uncle of mine, Lucien Chauvet, and they live in les Couguieux, the ancient Mr Archinard house!

Mr Archinard, who lived in your house once upon a time, came from St-Jean de Royan, in the Vercors, and began here as a garde-champêtre. (I think that is rustic policeman in English?) To increase his earnings, he used to do some seasonal agricultural works at my grand-parents' cultivation, and he used to eat with them every day, telling them the story of his difficult youth in the Vercors where he learned all about forests, and also where he learned to ski. He taught ski to my mother who was born in the early fifties, to give you a clue about the period. (She always said he was très à cheval when he was skiing—I think you would say he used the straddle position a lot? Kneeling?) He wrote poetry and was a photograher too, for he was journalist for the paper, Le Provençal. And the funny and interesting part is that he was a musician like you, Ruth! He played in the Philharmonique de Mazan, and he loved to sing and used to do this as often as possible. He was a truly kind and honest person and he knew the Ventoux better than anyone else. It seems like he knew all the botanical names of the flowers, plants and trees. That's why he was a guide for excursions in the Ventoux organized by the Syndicat d'Initiative for twenty years or more. Now there is a path named after him. He should have been proud of this.

Now, Les Couguieux—the house where you live, where lived Mr Archinard, his wife and their two sons— was the one where my grand-grandfather was born. It looks like it was a very rudimentary house where winters were very, very hard. And so, as a child I must have passed your house maybe ten times a month! And now I find myself on a site of someone who lives in the US, only to learn that my neighbours are English talented people living in the house where my grand grand father was born! This world is so small.

Anders Lazaret, illustrator, Les Baux, Vaucluse, France

The Key

ON MAY THE FIRST, with a little bribery and a lot of
patience, Julian put the last twenty thousand euros for
the purchase of the little house at Les Couguieux on a Visa
card. Then, amid much Provencal pinging and panging, the
regally chignonned Mademoiselle Clémentine handed the
key over to its new owners.

'You will be happy there,' she said.

'That's what everyone says,' said Julian. 'I hope so.'

The key was colossal. As long as my hand. It was thick
and cool, with a heart-shaped space at the top and two
simple ridges at the bottom where it would turn in the lock.
There was no duplicate. There was no 'this is the back door,
this the garage, that the pool house, and these for the window
locks.' There was One Key. I wondered, if we were ever to
replace the old door, if we would have to give up this instrument whose touch, in a pocket, would have been that of
home to a man wandering back from pruning or chopping or
singing in the local choir; from church, skiing, or a midnight
walk on the mountain. Who had fashioned it, I wondered.
What sound would it make as it met the lock? Would the fit
be snug or loose? Would it have alerted a man that he had
to put his pencil down? Or a woman that it was time for her
lover to leave? Would it turn silently?

'You must be prepared to replace the septic tank,' said

Mademoiselle Clémentine, waking me from my dream. We ignored her and said our goodbyes. Our transaction was intimate enough, apparently, to have turned cool handshakes into pecks on the cheek, and I do believe Mademoiselle Clémentine's was damp with a tear. We wound our way back toward the car, stopping en route for a raspberry tart and eating as we walked.

Carpentras was an odd town. We neither liked nor disliked it. I called it drab and Julian called it workaday. We had tried changing our allegiance to the fancier and equidistant Vaison la Romaine but we always came back. It had one of the best cheese shops in the country. It had our beloved *Marchés de Provence*, where the seasons were forever on abundant display and where Julian found most of his still life subjects. It had a world-famous truffle market and two excellent patisseries. Despite consisting of an unremarkable old centre belted in by a ring road, it had a diverse population and a rich (but not always proud) history. It boasted one of the oldest synagogues in France, built when, during the twelfth and thirteenth centuries, roughly ten per cent of the population were Jewish. The Jewish cemetery was famously and appallingly desecrated in 1990 by members of the National Front, whose leader, Jean-Marie Le Pen, enjoyed his largest following in the area. Because of its large North African population, the market was lively and the coriander plentiful. There was a chapel that hosted the occasional exhibition. There were a couple of festivals that seemed not to have gotten off the ground and a small music school that wouldn't consider my curriculum vitae, master's degree and half a doctorate from a prestigious New York university notwithstanding. Sometimes I would turn a corner and find myself in an old square thinking 'one day this will be renovated, and the whole town will follow, becoming the hub of Vauclusian cultural life.' Light flooded down the street now, the stone shone bright, a café buzzed. A poster advertised a Malian musician I particularly admired. It was not a beautiful town but it was our town and, after all, something happened in your relationship to a place when you were walking from the notary's where you had signed the deeds on a house.

'Thank you,' I said, biting into the layers of *sablé* pastry, *crème pâtissière*, and tart raspberries in their jelly.

'For what?'

I felt the key in my pocket. It was warm now. I never wanted to let it go.

'For leading me to the foot of the magic mountain.'

When this key appeared on my screen, I fell for it. We had a key just like this one for the outer gate, in Brazil, when I was a child. So I was back to Proust again, searching for lost time. Seeing this key was like Marcel's madeleine. Memories started seeping, and then flooding in—the feel of the key, its initial coolness warming up in my hand, its fitting into the green gate key-hole as if it knew exactly what it was doing. (The gate would open, and could be left open all day, allowing family. friends, or visitors to enter or leave.) Its perfume of iron, even, returned to haunt me.

Joyce Lowrie, prof. in French emerita, Wesleyan, Connecticut, USA

Cherries from M. Chauvet's Orchard

I am of French heritage. The Foisie family has been traced back to the Champagne region in the 16th century, from there over to Trois Rivieres, halfway between Montreal and Quebec, in Canada, and then down into New Hampshire in the U.S. I am also a still life and plein air painter. I only paint indoors when it rains. The daily paintings remind me that others are struggling to portray light as it falls on a bowl of cherries.

Annette Foisie, painter, Monterey, California, USA

'MAY IS GLORIOUS!' Julian said before my first spring. 'Provence is totally infused with colour and scent.'

Unfortunately, neither of us experienced the emerald month that year. While day-glo poppy heads nodded in blue fields of wheat, and pouches of broom released their perfume into the air, we neither saw nor smelled a thing. Our eyes were smarting from dust and our noses filled with spiders' webs. Habitable, my arse, I thought as we collapsed at the end of each day of dumping and scrubbing with a takeaway pizza and a vat of wine. Rather than cycling through orchards as I had imagined we would be doing, we were riding to and from DIY shops, their names all derived unimaginatively from the words *matériaux* and *bâtir*. On an exceedingly tight budget, our conversation had deteriorated into a scintillating comparison of prices of pipes (easily, we discovered, mistranslated as blow-jobs) and cables.

'That pipe was only three euros a metre at Baticrap!'

'No, it was four. It was three in Crappimat!'

'We'd better go to Batidepot quick then, and see if we can get it for less.'

'Which one was Batidepot? The one opposite Matéri... bollocks.'

The house we had fallen in love with and on which we had spent our entire savings had one fuse, two wires covered in burnt paper, an occasional trickle of running water, and a stinking antique septic tank to which we had no legal right. Our hands were so chapped by lime that the touch of a brush or a bow was but a distant memory, the only tools we knew how to handle being a corkscrew, an IVF needle and a pickaxe. Meanwhile, Julian's humming repertoire, reduced to three phrases from two middle period Beethoven sonatas and one hymn, was driving us both mad.

The locals passed us by in white vans, peering in disbelief. Monsieur Chauvet was the first to stop. He slowed down, got out, leaned against his bonnet, one hand on his waist, and examined us closely.

'I have been told about *les artistes Anglais*,' he said. When he spoke I could smell aniseed on his breath.

I extended a hand. 'Yes, I'm afraid we are taking over. Do you live here?'

'My wife's family were born in this hamlet and I live in Bedoin but I am from far away, a village called Entrechaux. Have you heard of it?'

Julian nodded in recognition of the village several kilometres from ours where we regularly dined with George and Jo and laughed. 'So you are a foreigner too?'

'Ah yes,' Monsieur Chauvet said, his eyebrows arching above his distant gaze. 'Yes, unfortunately, yes.'

We chatted for a few moments about the abundance, thanks to the canicule, of cherries in his orchard this year. 'Please help yourself,' he said, waving his hand vaguely southward. 'I am too old to pick them, and you know I am not well.'

In the garage, Monsieur Chauvet pointed out the manger behind our boxes of books and our cycles, and the hole in the loft above, from which the hay would have been dropped. He showed us his truffle orchard. He told us about the ochre caves behind the property that were used, in the past, to keep *le ving* et *les cochongs* of the troglodytes and, gazing over to the mountain, he talked about a certain Monsieur Archinard who was, alas, no longer with us, but who had known and loved the Ventoux better than anyone.

'What would the Provençal pronunciation of Les Cougieux be?' I said when he came to a stop.

'Well, Madame, it is spelled wrong on the sign.' He pointed to the authentic looking plaque on our wall. 'The mayor put this up for the tourists, but in Provençal the missing u makes the g hard: 'Cou-gui-eux.'

As he sang out the three rather than two syllables of our hamlet's name, now with a Siciliano rather than a marching rhythm, the voices of Jacques and Yvette Grouiller were forgotten in an instant, and in what felt like a ritual renaming of our four walls, we were back in the romance of Jean de Florette.

That evening we followed the earlier wave of his hand. We wove across meadows, between blooming grasses and wild orchids, and found ourselves in Lucien's orchard. From the thirty or so trees with their ringed mahogany trunks dripped pairs, threesomes and foursomes of crimson globes.

Three Cherries on a White Cloth

My friend Lucile and I have known each other since we
were sixteen and we get the giggles over cherries. Every
year we send each other something to do with cherries.
I found the best glass cherries in Murano. Once she sent
me a postcard she found in the Louvre with two women
in an opera whose nipples were cherries. Now we both
have cherry paintings by Julian.

Gilmer Edmunds, jack of all trades, Richmond, Virginia, USA

'VOUS AVEZ GROSSI,' said Monsieur Bigonnet, the fertility doctor. Although we had both gained a few kilos,
the French for you have put on weight sounded like you are
gross. 'We will give you a laparoscopy and clean you up. I
have had a look at your tests, Madame, but your eggs are
like those of an old woman. They are not good, but we can
try. Your sperm is good, Monsieur. Golden in fact. Never-
theless, from today you are both to avoid alcohol, lose four
kilos each, and fuck at least four times a week. And you
must continue this practice throughout your treatment, your
pregnancy, motherhood... and well into your eighties. It is
wonderful for your health.'

'Tomorrow we are going on the Atkins diet,' I said as we
walked to the car. A roll of fat spilled out of the top of my

knickers. I tucked it back in. It popped right out again. The kilo a day of big black cherries from the seller we passed on our way from the studio to Les Couguieux was beginning to register. Or was it the hormones? 'No carbs. No sugar. My friend lost a stone in two weeks.'

'Potatoes?' Julian asked as he picked up a tiny wren's nest that had fallen from a tree.

I was in that state where everything from a hare crossing the road to a bunch of cherries is a sign. I decided the nest was a sign. 'This time I have a feeling.'

'Please don't get your hopes up. If it happens, it happens and it will be marvellous. But the painting is only sold when the money is in the bank.'

'No. No potatoes. No fruit. But you can have bacon and eggs and cream and cheese.'

'No cherries? In cherry season? In Provence, for Christ's sake? Apricots will be out next, and peaches... then figs... you expect me to paint them and then just throw them in the rubbish?'

'I suppose if you paint them you might as well...'

'I shall eat them whether I paint them or not, and I shall eat bacon, eggs, bread and cream too. And potatoes.' Julian opened the door of the car. He placed the nest on my lap and started the engine.

'Well I'm going to have a go,' I said.

'You're a loony.'

On our way back to work on Les Couguieux, I came face to face with temptation. Perched on uneven ground just after the Lavender Petrol Station was a cart with a green awning. On the awning hung a lopsided sign with a bunch of three cherries sketched in red and green magic marker, and the words: *'Cerises du Ventoux 3 euros le kilo'*. The Cherry Seller. Underneath the sign nestled punnets heaped with deep black fruit, and, in among them, a tin. (This was for honest customers should they need sustenance during siesta time when The Cherry Seller was to be found asleep under his cherry-picking hat in his battered Citroen van.) As we approached the van, open at the back and oozing juicy surplus, Julian slowed. We wondered whether or not to succumb to the daily sugar fix. I decided against it. The seller, however, seemed to have another idea and was waving us down. '*Bonjour*!' he said, hobbling toward our car as we drew up on the verge. He glanced inside. Then he reached into one of his boxes, picked out three cherries on a single stem, leaned in through the open window, and placed them very tenderly in the wren's nest. '*Pour le petit nid*,' he said. For the little nest.

Well, if that wasn't a sign, I thought, what was?

Turnips from our Garden

IT WAS EARLY SPRING 2008, a year after Lucien Chauvet's death. Along the length of the house now ran four wooden boxes in which grew the beginnings of four varieties of tomato. There were aubergines. There were salad leaves, chard and rocket, turnips and beets. A Sicilian gourd reached upward with its first rampant tendrils. Potatoes were planned, naturally. Every square of growth was punctuated with an organic insect repellent or bee attractor such as rosemary or marigold, and the vegetables were arranged in happy families. Carrots that loved tomatoes, tomatoes that loved basil, radishes that loved mustard and redwort pigweed. Julian tapped a packet and three seeds plopped into his hand. He took a pencil and created an indent for them in a pot the size of an egg cup. He let the seeds drop. He placed earth on top of them, sprinkled fine sand over them, and watered them from a great height. Next, he transplanted a row of lettuces, gathering earth around the seedlings as lovingly as if he were tucking a child in to bed. Then, looking as smitten with the yellow blooms as he ever had been with me, he picked four Lady Banks roses from the bush and walked them toward the studio. It was time, I decided, for my annual letter to the neighbouring farmers.

'Monsieur, Madame, it is spring time! I am writing to you because the season to plant flowers and vegetables is once again upon us! As you may have seen, we have succeeded in creating a little potager..'

(I loved this word for vegetable garden, that translated as 'soup making plot')

'..on our terrace. But we would love to plant more! Might you have a field, corner or parcel to rent or sell? It would please us greatly to receive a proposition from you. I hope you and your family are well.'

I did not hold out much hope. Last year Monsieur Granet said, 'I am in the cherries. Call me next week,' but when, a week later, presuming he was out of the cherries, I called him, he didn't know me or what I was talking about. Neither Monsieur Croulard, nor Monsieur Chauvet had ever responded. 'Do not give up,' said Nadine. 'You never know. Things change. People die. They go broke. Land changes hands, crops flourish or fail, fathers pass on to sons...' This year, it occurred to me as I clipped the four envelopes to the postbox with a peg, something had changed.

When I noticed the Chauvets' white van parked outside our house, I felt nervous. Perhaps our log pile was too close to their wall, or our tomato plant was crossing a boundary, or the paint-spattered tee shirts that hung over the communal path were limiting access to their property?

'I received your letter,' said Olivier. His mother, Lucien's widow, stood beside him, examining the boxes that constituted our garden. Her hands were joined behind her back as she stooped to sniff the honeysuckle, and she looked displeased.

'Oh yes,' I said. 'It's just that my husband is a painter...'

I could hear Julian scolding me in my mind: darling, not

81

everyone is interested in art and music. Some people have hard jobs to do. They are out in the wind and rain tending to their blighted crops or working on a production line. What are they going to want with some English geezer's paintings of turnips?

'... and he loves to garden, and would love to paint what he grows, as well as cook with it and eat it, and as you can see we already...'

'I am sure we can come to an agreement.' said Olivier.

'We followed the advice of your kind father this year, whose presence at Les Couguieux will of course be greatly missed, and picked many of the cherries in his orchard. We made delicious jam. White and red. Would you care to—?'

I stopped. Had he just said what I thought he had just said?

'For example, you could use the little piece of land by the truffle orchard, here.'

Olivier was pointing to the perfect plot. It was yards from our terrace and faced south. In it I could already visualize Julian tending to his seedlings, nurturing them, giving them plenty of compost in which to flourish and protecting them from the wild boar. 'What's for dinner?' we would say, as we walked around our potager with our scissors. Or indeed, 'what shall I paint today?'

'Oh, Monsieur,' I said, 'you have made our dream come true! My husband will be so happy! He will have his artist's garden at last! Would you like us to buy, or rent? How should we settle?'

Olivier waved his hand, just as his father had done, and said: bah!

'This is so very lovely of you. Would you come in and have a cup of coffee with me? Or can I offer you a pastis? A print? I would like to show you the paintings Julian did, of turnips from our garden, or indeed of your father's cherries.'

Just to say that I have fallen in admiration in front of your paintings. From time to time I myself take the risk of colouring a canvas for my pleasure. However I can see I have a long way to go before I can even approach the quality of your work. I hope that the little piece of land for your garden will be sufficient and I wish you courage and success in the planting of your flowers and vegetables.

Olivier Chauvet, Bedoin, France

Vines and Rain

When I was a child in the Okanagan Valley we had Italian neighbours who grew and cooked things beyond compare—I remember their arbour with its succulent green grapes hanging above our heads, and the perfume of them, and sitting underneath that arbour eating Maria's food, and if I have a palate, and I think I do, I owe it all to Maria.

Barbara Cruikshank, painter and writer, Vancouver, Canada

BACK AT THE STUDIO in Crillon le Brave the rent was building up. We couldn't get out of it because Julian had nowhere to paint at Les Couguieux. Julian had nowhere to paint at Les Couguieux because the house still did not have plumbing or electricity. We couldn't pay for a plumber or an electrician because the commissions hadn't been finished. The commissions hadn't been finished because Julian was busy being a plumber and an electrician. We couldn't stop paying the rent at the studio because the commissions were set up there... and so on. My suggestions to take a month off the renovation to complete the commissions, move out of the studio and put the money we were saving on rent toward the renovation did not go down well. They went down about as well as my suggestion to do a little bit of painting every day, to keep in shape and bring in a little cash. (I paint when I feel like it, not when my wife nags me.) The parallels I drew, somewhat foolishly, between my own hour-long warm-up on the cello and a daily painting exercise were shunned. (Did I have any idea what it was like to face a blank canvas?) I brought sunflowers in from the fields and plums from the market and placed them in pretty bowls and vases. Then, as winter started to fold us in, I bought quinces and walnuts. I turned music off and on and left spaces clear. I wrote desperate calls for help on forums: could someone please explain to me why discipline and daily practice didn't seem to feature in my artist husband's life? How was it possible to support a painter who never seemed to paint? I expected a rush of empathy from long-suffering wives but instead I got emails back from both men and women telling me to let the poor blighter go, allow him some fallow time for god's sake, trust in the process. They advised me to stop being so manipulative, to take a look at my own creative life and examine what frustrations I was projecting onto him. I knew the people on the forum were right, but I couldn't help myself screaming at him inwardly, and sometimes outwardly. 'Why don't you just paint?' I said. 'Why don't you just shut up,' he said, seeing The Look cross my face. 'Trust me. I'll get a job if I have to.'

Summer came and went in a stupor of DIY and sweat. We stopped doing IVF. We continued paying the rent. Monsieur Bellon died. And still the celebratory bottles of Chateau this and that came. Celebrating what? I thought. Three non-symbolic cherries?

'Cheers!' said Julian. 'To our wonderful life!'

Old Grenache

Looking at today's painting of grapes I am reminded that there was a store here in Rockland, called the Wine Seller. The woman could have sold the Brooklyn Bridge. She had marvelous descriptions of each wine, and one day she said, 'This one is like taking a bunch of grapes in your hand, standing in the sunlight, squeezing them and letting the juice run down your arm.'

Nancy Warren, Rockland, Maine, USA

I DROVE OFF THE MAIN ROAD at Châteauneuf du Pape and on to an unnamed dirt track. On either side of us the hectares of vines stood, in their winter nakedness, like the orderly rows of a military graveyard.

'Where are we going?' said Julian.

It was Julian's birthday and I had booked a treat.

'Secret,' I said.

The château, reached through a rusty gate and along a length of tarmac bordered with frost-bitten rosemary, was small and unimpressive. More like a farmhouse. A flesh-coloured render covered the original stone. The windows were double glazed with plastic frames. Herbs had gone to seed in plastic window boxes. I found it hard to imagine the bottles leaving here and ending up on starched white linen in New York or Tokyo. However, on the metal door was a bell and next to the bell was written the name. This was it.

'Château Rayas!' cried Julian. 'How did you get an appointment here?'

I rang the bell. I didn't know what I had imagined, but the sound was weak and tinny. I rang again. No one stirred. I had, I said, booked a tour and tasting for ten o'clock. Perhaps we were early? Perhaps it was the wrong day, or he had forgotten? We decided to give it fifteen minutes before phoning.

Emmanuel arrived as if by accident to find us perched on the step dialling his number. A frayed flat cap sat like a weight on his head. Without apology or ceremony, he led us round the back of the building, slid the lock away from the oak door and ushered us into his alchemical cave. Taking three dusty glasses from a rack that hung just inside the entrance he spoke to us for the first time: 'I will keep you company.' His voice boomed in the glacial chamber. He beckoned for us to follow him up a rickety staircase. In a room full of stainless steel vats, he poured wine from a hose into our glasses, and then he began to talk. He explained that this particular white was composed of grenache blanc and clairette grape varieties, and that it would be ready to drink in twenty years' time.

'However,' he said, 'you can already get a sense of its potential in the empty glass and the empty mouth.' He pulled air in through his throat, made a whistling sound, spat and smiled.

'So you are a cellist? My wife and I love music and all my kids play.'

He took another slug, swilled, spat, and led us into the cellar where the reds were kept. There he took up a mallet and giant pipette and, turning the tap, explained that each of the barrels from which we were going to now taste held the fruits of eight different parcels of Grenache grapes. He pointed out of each of the four windows, with traffic-signalling arms to indicate their whereabouts, took another mouthful and swallowed.

'A good year of this,' Julian whispered to me, 'will set you back £859.57. I looked it up on the Web.'

'A string quartet would cost him about the same,' I whispered back. 'Maybe one day we'll be able to barter? Cheers. To...'

'To me. Happy birthday to me!'

Emmanuel sucked the liquid into his pipette and dropped it into our glasses.

'The parcels facing the sunrise,' he explained, 'will taste of red berries, the sunset parcels of tobacco. They will be skilfully blended, bottled in the spring, and released the next year.'

I watched Julian as he plunged his nose deep into the glass, swirled, inhaled, gurgled and spat. He barely held the crystal, as if it were a ball to which his fingers were listening for some profound truth. The wine was reflected in his cheeks, his eyes were closed, and on the translucent semicircles of his lids I could see the vein structure. I knew his tongue was swollen with pleasure.

'We often talk of having a concert here one day,' Emmanuel said.

Julian opened his eyes and looked at me. We smiled.

We finished the tour and as we were preparing to leave, Emmanuel asked Julian the year of his birth. When Julian answered, Emmanuel took a black marker from a shelf. In an elegant French hand, his figure 1 sporting an extravagant tail, he inscribed Julian's birth year on a label. Then he cut the label and handed it to Julian along with an empty bottle.

'Here. For your paintings. It was a good year. I hope this

is a good year for you. When you are famous you will come and buy a case from me to celebrate!'

Julian thanked him.

'And you, Madame... It is my wife's fortieth birthday next year. We would like to celebrate. Would you play for us and a few friends at our home?'

'I would be delighted,' I said.

Saucisson and Bread

I purchased The Lido in Venice for my husband as a reminder of our time at the Danielli over twenty years ago, a first vacation together after the birth of our daughters, a time of rediscovering 'us' in the liquid, grey winter light of Venice.

Hope Schneider, partner in thought, La Canada, California, USA

ALTHOUGH JULIAN AND I MET in 2000, it is just possible, because of our shared passion for food, we bumped into one another many years before that. In a little Italian deli on London's Old Compton Street.

It was 1984. I was nineteen. I was renting a small room in a big north London house, wearing shocking pink Doc Martens and eating brown rice. I was travelling back and forth to Duesseldorf for cello lessons and knew little of Mediterranean cuisine. Although Elizabeth David's classic Italian Food had been in print for thirty years, its recipes had not made it to my bedsit. I had heard of spaghetti and was quick to buy the pretty green-ridged jar in which to store it, but secretly I thought of it as something that required an alien fork technique and sucking noises. Then came my first professional gig. A month in Venice. Suddenly my world opened up. Suddenly I was playing real music in a real orchestra, floating in sandals over moonlit bridges and eating pumpkin ravioli. After Venice came tours in Modena, Lucca, Amalfi and Bologna; in-between, London felt dreary. There was no Carluccio in those days. No Jamie. The River Café would open only in three years' time. There was just a little shop in Soho, on Old Compton Street, called I Fratelli Camisa. There, after Ravenna and before Pesaro, my colleagues and I would huddle. Only there, we agreed, could we get Castigliani pasta, Contadino unfiltered olive oil and copious quantities of fresh basil. Only there was the parmesan 'really Reggiano' and only there could you buy a proper Italian pizza-slicing wheel.

A couple of years earlier Julian had graduated from Wolverhampton Polytechnic with a bachelor of arts degree (which, as far as I can understand, was in creating photomontages of himself measuring fields with the length of his body) and moved to London. After a stint washing the floors of the city's first McDonald's, he was offered the job of manager of the independent cinema the Lumière in Soho. He took it. Mostly he took it in the belief that, while tearing ticket stubs for Dream of Light and Jean de Florette at night, he would, during the day, be free to pursue his own dream of becoming a conceptual artist. However, late nights in Frith Street's Bar Italia proved more enticing than sitting in a small room in the suburbs trying to become a painter and, as he says about that period of his life, it was easier not to. Besides, what was there to bloody paint in Brockley? So, instead, he absorbed. At home he absorbed harmony, texture, colour and balance through his love of food, from wrapping up a potato curry in a chapati and eating it with his hands (techniques acquired after his years in the Indian and Pakistani communities of Wolverhampton), to experiments in nouvelle and Mediterranean cuisine. At work he absorbed light, motif and form through the great masters not of paint, but of film; from the frames created by Hitchcock, Bergman and Tarkowsky that he projected night after night. And in his breaks he often walked, his Paul Smith jacket slung over his back, two blocks from Saint Martin's Lane down to Old Compton Street. There he stopped at a little Italian place he knew called I Fratelli Camisa, which sold most excellent sausages.

'Those big meaty ones,' Julian said. We were standing now in the organic butcher's shop, in Caromb, both in no-name unisex fleeces, shorts and Birkenstocks, watching the father and son team flirt with the customer before us over the exchange of three faggots and a five euro note.

'Did you go there around lunch time, because I often went late morning?' I said.

'You know, those ones with string…?' said Julian.

In 1997 Julian was made redundant from the cinema. The building that housed the Lumière morphed into a Philip Starck hotel that boasted interactive light installations in the bedrooms, and Julian was handed a cheque, along with a crate of Artificial Eye videos. He took his money, his films and his chance, and decided, once and for all, that he was going to be an artist. He left the London home where in the kitchen he had built the cupboards and carved the knobs from rosewood, where in the garden he had planted the bleeding hearts and the rosemary, and fed the fox, and where the walls had protected Colin the cat, housed two long-term relationships, and hidden one affair. He took his easel and paints, and drove his gold Citroen Visa down to his writer friend Gary's house near Crillon le Brave, on a one-way ticket to find his muse. By then I was living in Brighton. I had an occasional French sailor in tow. I had swapped DMs for deck shoes and striped sweaters, and the Italian dream for a French one that played itself out in La Rochelle and Paris. Julian and my chance of meeting in an Italian deli in Soho had now become an improbability. However, I had met a girl, and that girl's brother was a writer living near Crillon le Brave...

'Despite my love of sausages with string, I've only been once to Italy,' said Julian.

Father butcher handed his customer her package, winked, and asked if she had any other desires.

'Over the border to Ventimiglia with my friend Nick. The coffee was good, as I remember, but it just seemed like this crazy place to us. Full of old women in black wandering round with chickens. So we came back.'

'It's only three hours' drive from our house,' I said.

'Mademoiselle?' said the butcher's son. 'What is your pleasure?'

I was flattered by his form of address. 'Two of your marvellous sausages please. You know you have the most marvellous sausages in the whole world?'

'But even with the best sausages in the world we haven't seen you here recently,' said the butcher's son. 'Do you not love us any more?'

'We have bought a house,' I said, 'and unfortunately it is in Bedoin. A bit far...'

'And are you going to invite us to your *cremaillère*?' said the son.

'What is a *cremaillère*?' I said.

'It is when you invite everyone to your new house and all the men get drunk on pastis and sleep with all the other men's wives.'

'Well,' I said, not sure if we were quite ready for this kind of celebration. 'Of course you can come to our *cremaillère*. When we have it. So long as you bring your sausages...'

'Ah, Mademoiselle,' said the son. Above the counter two bald heads glimmered bronze in the fluorescent light as father and son nodded sagely. 'We never go anywhere without our sausages.'

Giudecca Sunrise

*It was 1974 and I was on a train, traveling from the north
to the south of Italy. I was sitting on my suitcase in the
aisle, sharing a roasted chicken with an old man who
was naming things for me as they passed by the window.
Farms, villages, grasses. There was a blaze of carnations.
Then there were fruit trees. I was so happy I wanted to
leap from the train and walk amidst flowers, reach up
and pluck a pear, raid a chicken coop for an egg or two.
Julian's paintings remind me of that day.*

Madonna Hitchcock, Baltimore, Maryland, USA

IN ZECCHI, ON FLORENCE'S VIA DELLO STUDIO, Julian
looked upon paint tubes with as much desire as he had
looked upon the pistachio torte in the baker's window earlier
that day. In fact, the *verde di cadmio chiaro* had, he observed,
a distinctly similar hue to the cake we had just shared.

We had come from the Uffizi. Julian had trotted through
the galleries apparently untouched until, arrested by Raphael's self-portrait, he stood and wept. Now, in the famous
fine art shop, he was remembering that painting. He gazed
at the pigments laid out on the shelves: raw Umber, burnt
Siena and Napoli yellow. We had driven, he mused, across
the Umbrian earth upon which Raphael had stepped. We

had dined and slept the previous night in Siena, whose soil's pigment had most likely become that of of the artist's eye in his self portrait. We would soon pass through Napoli, a hint of whose sunny *terra*, surely, was in the portrait's skin tone? We murmured the names together, *terra d'ombra naturale, terra d'ombra bruciata, terra verde*. Pigments of the earth, the earth of a country I had loved for so long and that now, clearly, already had Julian in its thrall. And we hadn't even reached Venice!

We arrived on the Giudecca just as the autumn sun breathed out its last on the Venetian lagoon. A cruise ship was pulling in at the same time. It dwarfed the Santa Maria dome and the arches of San Marco. Our vaporetto curved around it before letting us down at Palanca, the unglamourous side of the lagoon on which we had rented a friend's apartment. We passed a row of shops selling mortadella, mozzarella, chicory, lightbulbs, toothbrushes, octopus and dry bread. We turned right in to our liquid street and walked to the trattoria above which we were to stay. We put down a rucksack, an easel and a paper bag of Zecchi paints and we knew, as soon as the key clicked in the lock, what we were going to do. Julian was going to paint, and we were going to cook!

We soon established a rhythm in which a visit to the Rialto market became a form of daily worship. We took our shopping trolley across the lagoon on the vaporetto, walked it through the streets, hiked it on to the public gondola and crossed the Grand Canal with it. Then we filled it up with razor clams, shrimp, porcini mushrooms, flowering zucchini, curlicues of Treviso radicchio, and leaves. And, of course, sausages with string. The bar on the adjacent square did little sandwiches—salt cod, cured ham and radicchio—which we devoured, along with a glass of prosecco, at whatever time we finished shopping, and called it lunch. Weighed down further with a couple of bottles of soave or friuli wine we made our way back. We wandered through leafy campos and alongside canals reflecting sea green boats and houses of crumbly red bricks, over wooden bridges and past gondola repairers and book binders. We paused to rest and read menus. Everywhere the light danced, on canapes and hanging vines, and in the ripples made from the water traffic. People hung upside down in the canal as they crossed over the *ponte* Santa this or into the *fondamento* San that. Our load became heavy. We stopped again for more prosecco, standing on a paper-littered floor and watching the water lick the stucco from the bottom of a building or laughing at the fennel boat just missing the rubbish boat and bumping in to the post boat. Back at the flat the razor clams met the boiling water and split from their shells. Their engorged tips poked out and waggled like excited members. We feasted on them, digesting all that we had seen and smelled that day. After lunch Julian spread a protective plastic layer over our friend's dining table and started to paint. By the end of the week we had put on six pounds and he had six purple paintings.

Dusk, Grand Canal

I was searching for 'paintings of fruit' as a way to tie Renaissance folks like Arcimboldo to our modern day art world. Instead, I found Julian.

Amy Degerstrom, prof. of art history, Duluth, USA

OUR LAWYER, BERNARD, was getting impatient. Two iris seasons had now passed since the sale of Julian's London flat, for which Bernard had agreed to be paid with a painting of his favourite flower, and Julian's side of the bargain had not been upheld.

> From: Bernard@withersanddraper.co.uk
> Subject: my bloody still life
>
> julinetta, i don't know if you are still waiting for a fresh paint delivery, or if having that woman over there full time is cramping your style. all i do know is that when this bloody iris painting is ready to be unveiled, it had better be good.
> Kissy kissy, Bernard

Julian replied immediately, explaining that Bernard was surely taking up more of his head space than he was of Bernard's. He promised that the painting would be delivered very soon, and asked where Bernard was going to hang it.

From: Bernard@withersanddraper.co.uk
Subject: my bleedin' irisetti

J, surely you haven't got time to respond to emails so
quickly?– shouldn't you be out there in the floral banks painting? I will hang it it in the office and see if I can drum up
some interest from the more discerning of my punters for
you. Listen, send me some other pictures and I may part with
some sterling too.

Bernard signed off with his usual playfulness, this time as
Mabel. Julian sent me off to the ridge urgently to pick irises.
Then he replied to Bernard, attaching one of his Venetian
scenes. He said that he realized Bernard liked purple flowers
so maybe he liked purple paintings in general, and if he did,
he might like to see another Venetian scene as they would
make a nice pair. When I returned from my walk, irises
bunched in my arms, Julian danced down to the kitchen to
greet me. His laptop was wagging in one hand as, with the
other, he cut himself a slice of the Provençal cherry dessert, clafoutis, he had made that morning. He read out Bernard's reply.

Julie bum. Venice is nice. Let's have a look at the other one,
but probably yep. You can bring them over when you bring the
still life masterpiece.

Julian spat out a stone. 'Did you hear the word them? Could
it be that he wants them both? Or does he mean the Grand
Canal and the irises? Will you read it for me? Here. What
do you think? Christ, I can't stand this.'

'Perhaps, yes,' I said, looking at the email. 'It could be
that he is considering…'

'More cake!' said Julian. Although there was still
half of one cake remaining, Julian set about preparing a
second. He twirled round the kitchen like a morris dancer

on a village green in between the beating of eggs. Then he replied to Bernard, attaching Santa Maria delle Salute at dusk and asking if Bernard still wanted purple irises to go with purple Venice paintings. He wittered on about how big the conveyancing bill was on our French house and ended his email with 'Please give me some clarity, and then I will tell you the whereabouts of a picture of Ruth wearing wellingtons.' An hour later, the buzzer on the oven went confirming the readiness of the tart, and a ping confirmed Bernard's purchase.

From: Bernard@withersanddraper.co.uk
Subject: santa maria's bleedin' tagliatelle irisettone

clarity?—from a lawyer?—are you trying to put me out of business? I confirm I wish to purchase said pair of venetians for 900 english pounds. I also wish to be provided with one iris still life in exchange for legal services rendered in connection with the sale of uk property but it will have to be bloody huge as the conveyancing costs have now gone up so that I can keep up with those frenchies. Now, I also need to talk to you about painting irises for my father.

Julian cut himself a steaming slice of the new cake. 'Today I have earned nine hundred pounds! I have also had two puddings!' He was hopping around the house giggling at a new reason not to paint. 'And I've got a new iris commission! I can't possibly work! I'm all tingly!' He tap-tapped his confirmation. He told Bernard the address of the family blog where the picture of me could be viewed and added that if, in the case of another family member having posted recently about tv or church or whatever, a light scrolling motion would make 'the buxom beauty' (me) appear.

'Let's go out to dinner tonight,' he said. 'We will have potatoes and more puddings and we will drink champagne!'

'Let's finally give Madame Bellon notice,' I said, 'pay the rent, and move to our new home. And then have champagne.'

'But I'm fizzing....!' said Julian.

Approaching Rain

I have lived most of my life on waterways, on the Hudson River, the Atlantic Ocean, Lake Michigan and now the Gulf of Mexico, which is why I particularly enjoy Julian's water scenes.

Grace Snyder, children's clothes designer, Sarasota, USA

A T LES COUGUIEUX we received a letter from the water board and the news was not good. I brought the document back with us to Crillon and now I read it out, translating as I went.

'We understand that you are the new owners of this property and we would like to alert you to the fact that your house, parcel number seventy-four on the plan, has no waste water system. Such a system, when it is installed, needs to conform to the rules set out by the waste water board (please see attached… doobrie-whatever) and needs to be five metres from any boundaries, fifteen metres from any… I think that means banks, five metres from the house, three metres from any trees, thirty-five metres from any wells or springs used for drinking water —'

I broke off. 'How many metres do we have in front of the house?'

'Seven by three giving onto a road and a boundary. Go

on,' said Julian.

'We would also like to inform you that the land attributed to the property is insufficient to install such a system.'

'In other words, we have nowhere to put our poo. What else does it say?'

I skimmed the contents. 'Well, there are a lot of long words like *assainissement* and *dimensionnement*. Lots of *indispensables* and *impératifs*...but basically it says that we are fucked unless we can persuade our neighbours to sell us some land. It is signed by a—wait for it—you won't believe her name! a Madame Badoit.'

'Peasants never sell their land.'

'And it says that we have to do a soil test and send them a thousand euros.'

'What's the point of a soil test if we haven't got any soil?'

Outside the house in Crillon the beginnings of a storm were crackling in the air and we went out into the waiting street to see if this time the drought would break. The parched cobbles in the alleyways gaped up at the moonless sky and shutters struggled to be free from their catches. The air was as thick as bouillabaisse. The lightening took panoramic snapshots, illuminating steeple cages and blue hills. Then, urgently, the downpour came. All four seconds of it. We listened to the wetness slapping at our sandals and watched the steam rise from the pavement. Mme Bellon, her yellow print dress already heavy on her hips, was dragging her flower boxes in toward her porch when she stopped to touch the skin on her arm in disbelief. I made a gesture to indicate my gratitude to the heavens for the gift. She said that what we had just witnessed really was only *quelques gouttes*, and that we needed much more than a few drops to stop six years of drought. She said the heat of the *canicule* had done so much damage to the crops this year that many would not survive, the rivers had run dry, and that old folk had died. The alcohol level in the wine would be high and morale low. We stood together for a while, waiting. Then we kissed and said good night and went back into our houses.

'There must be an environmentally sound alternative to the septic tank,' said Julian. 'I'll do some research.'

'I'll book an appointment with Miss Sparkling Water,' I said.

Madame Badoit was late for our rendez-vous and I had to listen to the water feature for forty minutes before she clip-clopped in.

'Thank you for meeting me,' I said, offering her a hand which she refused.

We ascended the three flights to her office and as we did, I became mesmerized by a bunch of hair wagging at me from her cranium. Once we were seated in the plasterboard cube, I explained the situation. We had been using a septic tank on the ex-owner's brother-in-law's land, which use he, the ex-owner's brother-in-law, was now withdrawing. We had received her letter, and understood the principles, but we clearly could not put in a septic tank of our own as we did not have enough land. Any land, in fact. However, and here was the good news, my husband had found a water treatment system that met the European norms: N1256.

'What does it say in your bill of sale?' Madame Badoit was picking through some papers on her desk. 'Here. It says clearly that you have no right to the septic tank and that you must install one of your own. You should have read this before you purchased, Madame.'

'But you do not seem to have heard me, Madame. You yourself say in your letter that we do not have enough land. We want to talk about what alternatives there might be.'

'You do not seem to have heard ME, Madame. You have no alternatives. You must buy the vines opposite your house.'

'But Madame, they are not for sale.'

'Then I will write an official letter to the owner, Madame, demanding that he make them for sale.'

'But this system, Madame, that my husband has found... you know we are in a drought here in the Vaucluse and that water is very precious. We can put it directly in front of our garage and we will have clean water to give away! Next year it will be legal to use it as a toilet flush and in five years it can be used to fill swimming pools.'

'Who is selling it? Show me the information.'

'You have it in your hand. It is there, the blue writing, yes, that's it. It is a Monsieur Marin.'

'I have never heard of this system.'

I knew this was not true as Monsieur Marin had informed us during our phone conversation that he had already visited Madame Badoit.

'I will send you the letter. You will copy it and send it to all the landowners around your house. If no one will sell we will have to proceed to the next step. Then we will see. Goodbye.'

Autumn on the Rhône

In my childhood bedroom in Brookline, Massachusetts, there was a medium sized Constable of a small bridge in a green setting. I gazed upon it for many months and learned how to sit by a vertical stream of water. I still know how. This early impression resonates in the land-scapes Julian paints.

Peter Kaye, psychomusicologist, Santa Monica, California, USA

IT WAS MARKET DAY in the small town of Mazan and in among the nine stalls we spotted Monsieur Marin. He had a jet-black wig that was sitting crooked on his head, and he was holding a clipboard on which Give Water A New Life was written. His handshake was purposeful. The itinerary, he informed us, was Mazan, Bédarrides, Althen les Paluds and lastly Châteauneuf du Pape.

'And,' he said, bursting into laughter, 'we are going to be inspecting shit!'

As the car drew up alongside the first mini water treatment plant, we saw the proud owner planting box hedges on its perimeter. Marin got out of the car and shook his client's hand with a vigorous chopping motion. He opened the system's lid and showed it to Julian in action. The first chamber, he explained, was the place where the suspended solids would settle down.

'Have you done any good shits today, Monsieur?' he said to his client in a secretive aside.

'Yes, an excellent dump today, thank you,' said the client pointing to the fourth chamber. 'My wife cooks such good food.'

'I can vouch for that,' said Marin. He winked and pointed to the second chamber where, he said, the aerobic micro-organisms grew, creating the biofilm.

'And she mixes a good cocktail too.'

He chuckled, adjusted his wig, and put his salesman's voice back on. He explained that the biofilm converted the organic and inorganic compounds into carbon dioxide and nitrate by means of fine bubble aeration. That was why, he said, the biofilm was somewhat fizzy.

'Like champagne!' I said.

'I have to admit,' Monsieur Marin was giggling again, 'I know some better ones in the region. Come, I will take you to the next plant.'

Julian looked at the client, at the first chamber and then back at the client. 'Sir, I pronounce you in most excellent health!'

Everyone laughed, shook hands, and we parted company. We piled back in the car and turned right toward Avignon. On the journey Marin explained to us about the corruption that went on at the water board. He said that the amount of sand needed to make the soakaway for a septic tank was considerable and that that sand had to be replaced every five years.

'That's a lot of sand,' he said, 'which means a lot of back-handers from the sand people, which is why the water board would rather dig up a crop than put in a mini treatment plant.'

He informed us that by 2008 all departments were supposed to have carried out controls on all private wastewater
systems. However, because they were charging, illegally, a
hundred and fifty euros for this 'service,' most people, right-
fully, were refusing to pay it. As a result, the departments
had, illegally, stopped the controls.

'The obligatory soil test,' he continued, 'before install-
ing a septic tank costs a thousand euros, a quarter of what
an entire mini treatment centre costs. What would you do?'

The next client we visited had a cabanon in Châteauneuf
du Pape. Traditionally these stone buildings were erected
on agricultural land to provide shelter for chickens, goats,
wine makers, and shepherds, and had access to neither water
nor electricity. Now, however, if they were not in ruins, they
were to be found done up as bijou weekend retreats. Sometimes, if building permission could be obtained, they were
even enlarged beyond recognition, becoming appendages to
grand homes with swimming pools. This particular cabanon, thankfully, had retained its modest character. It sat in
vineyards in which the thirteen priceless grape varieties grew
that were allowed to make up the queen of the Rhône wine's
character: Grenache, Syrah, Mourvèdre, Picpoul, Terret
Noir, Counoise, Muscardin, Vaccarèse, Picardan, Cinsault,
Clairette, Roussane, Bourboulenc. It was constructed with
the same stones that lay on those beds from which sprang
the Châteaux Beaucastel, Vieux Télégraphe, La Nerthe, and
of course Rayas, and it looked entirely content. In front of
the building were a few square feet of terrace, bristling with
new growth. Pots contained lettuces, beans, and tomatoes,
and trays sprouting seeds. Roses, clematis and the client's
own single Châteauneuf vine ran up the trellis. There was
clearly no shortage of water here.

'Like you,' said Marin, 'the client owns none of the

surrounding land. He received a letter from Badoit only a month ago insisting that he buy a hectare in order to put in a soakaway. Do you know how much a hectare of Châteauneuf vines is worth?'

We nodded gravely.

'To buy enough for a septic tank would probably have cost my client four times what his home cost. All so he could soak away his...' Marin paused, trying to think of yet another colourful way to describe fecal matter '...hmm... waste, the Badoit way.' Then Marin pointed to a grey disc in the ground in front of the lean-to.

'That's it,' he said.

I looked at the disc two metres in diameter and thought about our law-abiding neighbour at Les Couguieux, Monsieur Chauvet. Recently he had, probably on Madame Badoit's instruction, cut down half his olive grove to make a new soakaway for a septic tank which, in a matter of only a few years (once the French had caught up the rest of Europe), would be illegal. Had he been better advised he could have saved his trees, and tens of thousands of euros too, not to mention a small piece of the planet. Our entire hamlet could have shared a waste water treatment system that could have fed a vegetable plot fit for kings. At least for chefs.

'Looks like civil disobedience might be our only option. When can we start?' said Julian.

I didn't get Marin's last joke which translated, as far as I could tell, as 'as soon as your bottoms are hot,' but we shook hands on the deal anyway.

JULIAN'S WALNUT TART

Take about 800 gr of fresh walnuts. Shell and grind them coarsely.

Roll out the pastry dough of your choice to line an 11-inch tart mold.

Pre-bake for 15 minutes, lined with aluminium paper and pie weights (such as dry beans) in a 200 degrees centigrade oven.

Beat 250 grammes of heavy cream until thick.

Fold in 6 tablespoons sugar and the walnut meat.

Place the pan on a cookie sheet and bake for half an hour until golden brown.

Walnuts

I'm a cookery teacher, so the kitchen is my world. Julian painted lovely walnuts which adorn my kitchen shelf above the sink. The other day, the walnuts came alive and jumped right into a tart mold to be made into a yummy walnut tart. Then back on the shelf to look lovely again. They want their tart to be printed. If you don't eat the tart at one sitting, do not refrigerate. Keep covered with an upside down plate. It lasts several days.

Lydie Marshall, cook, Nyons, France

THE SUMMER HEAT HAD PEAKED, the swifts had begun their departure from Crillon le Brave and this year, with the rent paid off courtesy of Bernard, we prepared to depart with them. Julian had been working doubly hard at Les Couguieux. He had re-installed the hot water, which now dribbled through an expensive showerhead into a beautifully crafted en suite cubicle. He had laid new pipes. He had put sockets in useful places, replaced electric wires and installed three computer points, and he had created an exquisite adobe-style cat flap in the wall for Oscar and Manon, our adopted kittens. Though far from pretty, the house was at last safe and what we, not the estate agents, understood to be habitable.

We were loading the last fragile items into the car: two old English cellos circa 1772 and 1740, and two Dogon fertility statues from Mali that had travelled with me from London to Düsseldorf and New York and back, and to which I still did not quite understand my passionate attachment. Finally, twelve finished and twenty-one unfinished canvasses, and three Macintosh computers.

Julian paused in the street, a clamshell ibook under each arm, and looked up at the swifts wheeling around the church spire. Together we watched their scythe-like wings cutting though the sky apparently without beating. Without alighting and without making a footprint anywhere they made their way to Africa in one unbroken journey. Even their nests were made from materials gathered on the wing. Things grasped from thin air such as feathers, hay and seeds, and cemented with saliva. Each spring when they arrived, Julian shed a tear as he explained to me the birds' awesome task. He told me that the young sat at the nest entrance looking out for days, wondering if they were fit enough, if it was safe enough, if they had enough fat on them to fly. And then suddenly, one day, when the time was right, they just did it. They flew to the other side of the world.

Julian closed the boot on the fourth and final carload.

'I wonder where we will be be when they are over the Sahara. Will our sign be swinging outside the hamlet announcing Mallow Gallery? Merrow-Smith Fine Art? Le Hameau des Artistes?'

Will we have any plaster on our walls, I wondered.

'And what shall we call our home? Chateau Lavande? Chez Monsieur et Madame Badger?'

Madame Bellon appeared on her doorstep, ready for her early evening watering. 'Is this goodbye?'

'We were just saying how we will miss the swifts,' said

Julian.

'And I will miss having you next door,' said Madame Bellon, her liver-spotted hand trembling with the weight of the rusty watering can. We kissed and talked a little. We agreed that life in the village had changed irrevocably, that the number of souvenirs being left by Grouillers' dog, especially on foreigners' doorsteps, was unacceptable, and that the constant grate of their voices created stress where there used to be peace. She was sure it had been him who tacked a nail into our tyre the night of the storm.

'I liked it when the street was filled with the sound of birds and a cello. Anyway, you...' After seven years, she still spoke to Julian with the formal vous. '...have been...' I was waiting for her favourite word and there it was. She put the can down, wiped her hand on her housecoat and thrust it in front of her for Julian to shake. '... impeccable,' she said, her eyes sparkling with pride. When Julian leaned toward her, the proffered hand ended up somewhere between her breasts as the smells of thyme and turpentine mingled in their embrace. 'I pray for you both that you will have every success and above all, the joys of a family.'

Madame Bellon and I embraced too. Julian looked up at the window that framed Jacques Grouiller's scowl. He hugged Madame Bellon once again.

'Wait one minute,' Madame Bellon said, waddling back into the house.

She came back with a bottle. 'My walnut wine. Made from the fruit of the village tree, the tree under which you have sat for many years, the walnuts which you painted when you first arrived.'

The bottle was tall and dark and I noticed that the oil from the nut had given the amber liquid a greasy film. I took out the cork and, inhaling deeply, remembered how Julian would rub the leaves for me to smell when I first arrived. The most aromatic leaves of any tree, he would say.

'It is as good as any sauternes,' she said, 'and gets better with age.'

'You will visit us?' I said.

'Of course I will. Once you have settled.'

'And, if I do a concert in the village, will you come?'

Madame Bellon said nothing and I knew she didn't think it her place. We all knew also that, although we would only be in the next village, we might as well be moving to a different continent. Julian looked back up at the window where Jacques had been joined by a gloating Yvette.

'Au revoir Crillon le Brave,' he said and, as he had always done, he rolled the car down the hill in neutral.

Grapes and Fresh Walnuts

I receive my daily postcard in my home at the foot of the Dandenong Ranges, on the edge of a national park and near to many Australian wineries. From my kitchen window I hand feed kookaburras, and there are rosellas and sulphur crested cockatoos all around us. Sometimes I hear the little steam train up on the hill called Puffing Billy. That is just up the hill and Ruth, the CEO of Puffing Billy, is a Welshman who is a classically trained cellist.

Sophie Wajsman, Victoria, Australia

ON THE FIRST MORNING as full-time residents in our new home, we were woken by a different kind of light. It sliced in between the shutters and landed plumb on our eyelids. It was the kind of light that entered directly without knocking, that did not loiter in an alleyway or creep up a staircase but, like a maid in white starched cotton, came frankly into the room and announced the day. As he lay with me under the sheet, Julian reached into the rays and closed his fist around the light.

'A sunbeam for my love!' he said.

We got up, put on a pair of tee shirts, climbed over boxes, brewed our coffee and opened the door on to the vineyard. What a breakfast room! The rows of vines, heavy with their purple fruit, swayed in the breeze like an overweight chorus line. The contralto bottle-blow of a hoopoe floated on the air. A cuckoo repeated his hat-tipping greeting, a woodpecker made a sound like a ruler reverberating on a school desk and, as always, cicadas clacked. In the distance we could hear the bleat and bells of the goats and the 'trillup trillup' of the goatherd. So far we had neither seen nor heard a car.

'By the way,' said Julian, 'the guy in Long Island wrote again. I picked the letter up in the studio yesterday. Yes, an actual letter this time. It's been so long. I can never finish his summer snow painting. Shouldn't I just write to him and tell him?'

'Yes, I suppose so.' I choked slightly on my toast. 'What did he say?'

In front of us two straw hats bobbed in and out of the leafy sea as the grape-pickers bent and straightened. Behind the workers, on top of a small hill, sat a hamlet, its pale blue shutters closed like bruised eyelids against the heat.

'He was so good about it. He said he loved it so far, that there was no hurry, and he could advance me some more money. He seems like such a nice chap and he has very lovely watermarked paper.' Julian kicked his bare feet into the air. 'I can't think about that house right now. I can only think about this one. You do understand, don't you?'

'Yes.' I said.

I breathed deeply and tried to think about fallow time. Two church bells struck ten a hamlet apart.

'And Bonnie's grandchildren, did you see them this summer? They are looking so fine, but if I hadn't studied the structure their faces so hard a year ago I wouldn't have a clue which one was which.'

He looked over at me. 'I know you think I'm never going to do any work again but it's absolutely not true.'

Julian then proceeded in making a quick speech, swallowing half the words as usual. He said how excited he was about making the hayloft into a studio, how many paintings he was desperate to do, how he was going to submit work in to the Royal Academy Summer Exhibition and the Royal Portrait Society of London, how he was going to redesign his website, and possibly even create a new one. He would make prints and cards and calendars. And if only Croulard would sell or rent us a parcel of land, then we could grow everything we needed to eat and to paint. Cherries, peaches, apricots, turnips, beetroot, narcissi, roses, irises... perhaps we could even shoot our own wild boar.

We walked back into the kitchen together and as we passed the table I touched the walnut wine bottle. The glass was warm on the underside of my fingers. I spread them round the bottle for a moment and thought of Madame Bellon and her wishes for us. I noticed that the single sunbeam had become a river of light flowing in through the door.

Ochre Cliffs and a Patch of Blue

My little postcard is of the demoiselles' masses of red hair. I tried hanging it on the conical wall of the trullo in which I live. (I should explain that trulli are constructed like the bories of Provence. They are stone dwellings or storehouses with conical roofs traditionally built without mortar in order to avoid taxation, and are found the small part of the Pugliese countryside known as the valley of Itria. Some people describe them as Loire castles for hobbits.) Unsurprisingly the painting kept falling off the conical wall. Now it has found its place on a chest of drawers among all my miniature treasures. These are mostly from India, where I worked over a period of some years. Just on the left side of a Buddha there is a space where a tiny African soapstone passport mask nestles among shell and blue and green glass bead and brass necklaces. The whole is encircled by a twenty-two-foot-long string of ostrich-egg beads, bitten to their tiny shape by I guess what must have been a whole tribe of human teeth. Well, it's there that the demoiselles have happily chosen to finally let their hair flow down.

Jill Phillips, musician, writer, mum, Martina Franca, Italy

THE MEN FROM THE BBC crawled past the bar in Bedoin. They passed Le Tabac, La Poste, Le Brin de l'Olivier, the organic butcher and the traditional butcher, Vélo-Concept, Ventoux Bikes, Passion Coiffure, the two bad and the the one good bakery, and all the while with Julian's self-portrait staring out from inside their windscreen. Apparently, no one in the village knew the artist.

Julian and I were waiting for the crew of Wild Provence in the vineyard opposite the house. I in the boxy linen top Julian liked so much, and he in shorts and the only white tee shirt he could find not covered with brush-marks or red wine stains. We were excited. As we became progressively more drunk, we fantasised. As a result of his upcoming slot on primetime TV, the days of bag-in-box would come to an end. Our shelves would be stacked with Château Rayas. We would be able to make an irresistible offer on the ruin and Julian would finally have his north-facing windows. We would travel to see his brothers in Singapore and Africa, and mine in Bangkok. We would adopt thousands of babies from Mali and feed them truffles. The Cork Street and Madison Avenue galleries would be on the phone, the book would come out, the film would star Colin Firth...

The crew arrived two hours late. They opened the boot of their rental car. We opened another bottle of Viognier. They got out a huge furry microphone and a black box covered in knobs. Fuck! we thought, trying to stay steady on our feet.

I have no idea how we passed the screen test that day but, returning from a wedding party at three in the morning a month later, we got the message: 'We will arrive at eight tomorrow to start filming, and could we have a bit of cello to start?'

We were hung over, of course. We were both overweight

from a summer of aperitifs and, worse, the canapés that came with them. The shadows under our eyes were too dark for our years. Most of our clothes were covered with lime plaster. Outside our house there was a collection of rusty bed frames and severed toilets and inside there were three chairs, a wheelbarrow, a coffee machine and forty pairs of Birkenstocks arranged in a tower. Where were they going to film? The only solution, at least for the 'bit of cello' and perhaps for Julian's interview (although they had said they wanted him painting in a lavender field) was by the *Demoiselles Coiffées*, the natural ochre sculpture park a few dozen yards from the house.

I set up my cello in the crevice between two of the ochre forms. Just above my head, a carving in the sandstone informed me that Marc loved Nathalie. I started to play some Bach. I played very slowly, weaving my phrases in between the the sound of the cicadas. I watched the shadows of the pines as the sun shunted them over the many shapes of the cliffs. Observing the colours of the sand glow from green through tangerine and pink to deep red, I wondered if Julian would ever get tired of this shifting light. Occasionally I started listing the things I needed to pack for Salzburg (goggles, espresso maker, ethernet cable, running shoes, concert shoes, sports bra, concert bra, strapless bra, West Wing season 5, meditation CD, yoga mat, raincoat...) then I brought my attention back to the music. Julian, my favourite audience, sat at my feet, a tear balanced in the corner of one of his closed eyes. When I had finished the suite, I did a short interview, they arranged a time to interview Julian, and we all packed up. When we got back to the house one of the cameramen gave us fifty quid and bought a painting for his girlfriend. The next day I got on yet another aeroplane.

When I returned from the tour, Julian and I sat down to

watch the final cut of Wild Provence, which was to be shown on BBC2 over the winter. It started in a promising way, with the titles appearing over a hazy backdrop of Julian looking like a wildebeest painting in a lavender field at Sainte Colombe. Then it cut to the beekeeper and the harrier, and then the horse-whisperer. Finally we could hear the sound of the cello and we knew it was his turn. The camera panned in on my bow arm. Then it did a tour of the *Demoiselles Coiffées*. Then it did a tour of the curve of my cello's purfling, the shadow of the bow on the red sand and my bare feet. Then there was a prolonged shot of me banging on about the smell of thyme. Then, suddenly, the crew were in the Camargue riding white horses.

'Where are you?' I said.

'I guess I'm on the cutting room floor,' said Julian. 'I'm not very good when you're gone. I drink too much. I eat far too many potatoes. I must have looked wilder than any of the animals they were filming.'

We turned off the DVD machine and sat back on our chipped wooden chairs. Wild Provence, we realised, was not going to make our fortune. Not unless there was a market somewhere out there for middle-aged women playing Bach to the birds and the bees.

House with Blue Shutters

Question: how many still lifes does a man need?

Answer: One of lemons, hanging in our kitchen. One of oranges, hanging in our living room. One of a pepper and, er, a snail maybe, not sure, in our bedroom. One more of oranges, still not given to Doris, maybe for her birthday. One given to Iris by Julian. That one was seashells, I believe....

The olive market is nice. We're in Provence? Picking up my daughter's concert harp? We're driving around and happen upon an olive market (we may have seen it mentioned in a guide book and aim for it), an entire (small) town devoted to the olive for a day, or a week or something. With a jazz trio in the town square and, like, olives for sale. In every size and variety. And the ice cream shop has lavender ice cream which, it turns out, after you talk your children into it, tastes just like dirt.

Provence. The olive market. Summer. Jazz. You, or, rather, I, standing there with a dirt ice cream cone in each hand.

I buy a bouquet of big, fat artichoke blossoms for Julian and Ruth. I haggle with the flower guy, until he points out that I am suggesting paying double the price he

is asking. One of my favorite flowers, artichoke. Maybe
Julian will paint them, I think. That would be cool, to
see a painting by an artist I admire of something I have
touched. Then I wonder, wait, he's painted Ruth. Have
I touched Ruth? I shook her hand in Salzburg, I think.
Dude! Maybe I even got a hug! And we had cheese at
that triangular restaurant near that place... what was its
name again?

We have directions to their house, and instructions to
visit for dinner when we are in the neighborhood. Provence
in, what season is this, June I guess, Provence in June is
like the surface of Venus in the Ray Bradbury story, or,
at least, in the movie, raining, raining, raining, except it's
lavender fields instead of rain. There's so much lavender
you get tired of lavender, is what I'm saying. I don't know
this when I buy the ice cream.

We drive around in the Fiat Doblo with the harp in
the back. My wife says, Mig, ask someone where Bedoin
is and I say, I'm fine, honey, srsly, I have a map here, see?
And she says, no, I think we're lost and she shouts at
people, as we pass, 'Bedoin?' and they gesture back and
she shouts, 'Merci!' and says, 'I think they are telling us
to go straight.' Eventually our daughter, who happens
to speak French, has enough and asks directions for us.

We see a lot of Provence that afternoon. Turns out the
directions my daughter gets for us don't help much either,
although they do get us a bit closer. Vague memories,
through the mists of a migraine, of 1) drinking wine and
2) asking police officers for directions. Or maybe we ask
directions from wine-drinking policemen. Lots of driving
down roads that turn out to be driveways. A woman who
happens to be American is the breakthrough. 'Go straight
down this road here,' she says. 'You'll recognize the house

from the paintings.' No, she doesn't say that. She puts us on the right road, though, and sends us off in the right direction. The house, when I see it, I slow down and think, that looks like the one in the paintings. Thing is, I have this thought at every stone house we pass, and Provence has several. But there are people outside the house, and a barbecue is cooking away. And one of the people is Ruth, and one is Julian, so it's pretty obvious.

There are a lot of little roads in those hills Julian paints. They don't always show up in his paintings. This is maybe artistic license. But I have driven on all of them! So, like if they do show up in a landscape of his, that'll be another thing I've touched that he paints. They like the flowers. Julian puts them in a bucket, because they are too large for a vase. 'Maybe you can paint them sometime,' Ruth says.

'Dunno,' Julian says. 'Artichoke blossoms are hard.'

Bedoin abuts the surface of Mars, is a cool thing you might not know. I am wearing the nice shirt I brought on our harp-fetching trip, brought along because I thought, who knows, Ruth seems relaxed but Julian, who knows how posh he is going to be? A successful artist. Srsly. I mean, artist, maybe white tee shirt, maybe whatever, something nice. Maybe a three-piece suit. You never fucking know with artists. I am the only one with a shirt with buttons on it, it turns out, but not for long. The problem is solved when I spill wine on myself and Ruth throws the shirt in a bucket of water to soak and Julian gives me a shirt of his. Not the shirt off his back, strictly speaking, but identical to the shirt on his back: a white tee shirt. That's practically the same thing. Once I have Julian's shirt, I am as relaxed as everyone else. We eat chicken seasoned with herbs they pull straight out of the ground.

That impresses me as much as anything else. Honey, we need more thyme. Oh, okay [bend down, snip!].

It is a fragrant, delicious landscape, albeit a bit heavy on the lavender.

So we got to see their magical, old stone house, and drink a bunch of their wine, and take a walk to the surface of Mars, that strange, strange red miniature Monument Valley thing they have going behind their house. Has Julian painted that? All I know is the BBC filmed Ruth playing the cello there when they did their show on Julian.

What a place to live, next door to Mars, like that, among herbs. We left with new paintings, and a new shirt, and an old one covered in wine (didn't stain, Ruth! the soaking worked!), and new friends. We found our way back to our camp ground, and found our way home after that, and now I sit here typing this and wonder if I was ever there at all, really, or if this is just another false memory implanted by some forgotten book I really loved.

Michael O'Rourke, writer, Langenrohr, Austria

S HUTTER COLOURS were becoming an obsession. We spent afternoons driving around scoffing at the different shades people chose. Traffic light green, birthday candle pink and baby blue. Mostly, however, they chose lavender. Lavender, lavender, bloody lavender. When someone got the colour right, however, it was a different matter. Mulberry, olive, slate. These seemed to have the capacity to make mortar blush or cool the sky. Julian, still squeezing his artistic flair onto anything but a canvas, was determined to find the perfect colour. However, I could foresee years of suffering our current shade of Flaking Turd Brown before he came to a decision. One day, after two months of joint research,

I lost patience and sneaked out solo to buy a pot of paint.

'It's revolting!' shouted Julian from the top window as I got to work.

While his London walls were painted in subdued neutrals such as 'hay' and 'string' with the odd splash of turquoise, I had tried, and of course failed, to evoke Marrakesh's Majorelle gardens in my Brighton flat. Julian did not trust me an inch.

'It is the prettiest grey in the Vaucluse!' I chirped back from the ground.

'You don't understand how harsh the light is here. In this light that is battleship grey.'

'But I spent an hour with the assistant making sure the colour had just the right hint of lavender to soften it but not too much to make you sick, and enough blue to merge with the sky...'

'Yes, but you have to put it next to the ochre of the façade. It's the colour of the façade that is important. Not the sky. If you had a yellow façade this would look lavender but on a red one it just looks green'.

I started to paint the shutters anyway. I removed them from their hinges and laid them out on a trestle table in front of the house. In shorts and a bikini top, and moving the table at the same rate as the sun, I sanded them down. I coaxed filler from a nozzle into the gaping cracks in the old wood. Then I opened the tin and started to apply the paint. The brush made its oily way back and forth distributing the colour under the sapphire sky. The wood absorbed the hue as my skin absorbed the sun's rays. Swish, swish, swish...

It was only when I had been lulled into a deep state of meditation-on-blue that Julian screamed. Our terrace had, he said, become a fast-track for furious hornets flying low to avoid the mistral. He had located the double nest

in the hayloft and now he wanted to dismantle it with his
bare hands and some insect repellent. I insisted we call the
pompiers.

'They will kill you!' the two men shouted in unison as they
pulled up in their squat red truck. 'Two stings and you are
finished!'

The men watched in disbelief as the creatures blasted in
formation past my half-naked torso like fighter planes. As far
as I understood it, the pompiers were firemen, ambulance-
men and insect exterminators all in one. They rescued people
from mangled cars, extinguished blazes, rushed people to
hospital, rang out the death knell and, apparently, dismantled hornets' nests. They donned their protective clothing
and got to work.

It was six o'clock by the time they completed the exter-
mination and, since we were religious about our aperitif
hour, we offered the pompiers a pastis.

'*P'tit jaune?*' one of them said, relaying the invitation to
his colleague who was crawling out of his papery cocoon.

'Yes, that would be nice. A small one,' he replied.

Relaxing now at the end of the day with their yellow
pick-me-up, the men regaled us with their hornet tales: 'One
man managed to get stung twenty times. His head swelled
up to the size of a hot air balloon and he lost his mind! He
left his wife, went screaming round the fields at night... '
And, as if scared suddenly by his own story, the pompier set
down his glass, gathered up his uniform, got into his truck
and raced back toward the village, almost forgetting to take
his colleague with him.

I looked down the road after them, then up at the test
shutter now hanging on the ochre façade. Not enough
goddam lavender, I thought.

Cherries From Chauvet's Orchard

This is my lavender corner. The lavender in Julian's July 2005 painting matches the cover of Veranda magazine from the very same month, so there they both sit, next to a bunch of dried lavender from Provence.

Annette Larson, Europe Tour Operator, Atlanta, Georgia, USA

Quince Tree, Vines and Storm

Yesterday's painting was of quinces: we don't have too many here. A chap I work with brought me a quince one day but it was rather like a lumpy pear, overripe yet gritty and watery, tasteless and sort of rotting from the core. I liked its lumpiness and colour though.

My favourite encounter with a quince was the beautiful film El Sol del Membrillo. Quince Tree of the Sun. Also called Dream of Light. Perhaps you know it? It is a film about the Spanish painter Antonio López-Garcia trying to paint and draw his quince tree and all that happens. After I received yesterday's painting in my email I searched it out and looked at it once more. What was so vivid this time around was that Antonio smelled the quinces. Really smelled them. Took in their perfume. Took in their heft. Had a real relationship with them. And lo, that day in the local markets, there were quinces. So I smelled them too and understood why people love them.

Barbara Cruikshank, Vancouver, Canada

IT WAS THE END OF THE GRAPE HARVEST. The air outside was sickly with fermentation but, in our neighbours' home, burning pine cones scented the room and the first log fire crackled its welcome.

'What's with the water saga?' Nadine said as she fanned knives, forks and spoons out from the four place settings.

'The current mayor's brother,' Julian said, 'is the guy who is supposed to dig the hole for the treatment plant and we're not yet sure whether this is a good or a bad thing.'

'Good thing,' said Nadine. She was giving the final twirl to a Corsican sausage on a pitch-fork in the open flames. She crushed it with roasted garlic and smeared the paste over a slice of home-made bread. 'It's a good family. Cheers. To the *Hameau des Artistes*! May your stomachs be full, your souls happy and your waste water pure!'

'The problem as far as I see it is that the mayor's brother has never heard of such a system. If he finds out it is considered illegal by Badoit he might report us.'

Nadine now placed an earthenware tagine on the table. Lifting the lid she said 'I saw that Julian had painted the quinces from my tree and here they are for you to eat, in a lamb and quince tagine.'

Julian had taught me to love the imperfection of quinces; to preserve the dusty film on their lumpiness when I handled them because that was what made them interesting to paint. And yet I hated their dry taste, in particular I hated the Provençal speciality called *pâte à coings* (pronounced kwang) that was served with cheese in winter. I have to admit I was nervous.

'No, do not worry. The new mayor, Bonnet, is a good man,' said Nadine. 'The old mayor, Yvon Prudhomme, is a resident of Bedoin and he will be presenting himself as a candidate for re-election against Bonnet in March. He also happens to be the head of the water board.'

'Yvonne? A man and the mayor to boot?' I tasted the tagine. 'Nadine! One mouthful and you have made a quince-convert of me.'

Manuel ran a finger over the bronze buttocks of a sculpture he had clearly modelled on his beloved. 'And it's because of him that all this information gets twisted. That's why we are in the dark ages as far as the environment goes. It's his pockets that are being lined to keep it all quiet.'

'Of course it could turn out well.' said Nadine. 'Bonnet could get excited by the idea and spread the word, especially if it made people vote for him and gave his brother some extra cash each time a new one was installed... '

'Meanwhile,' said Manuel, 'did you know that Croulard wants compensation for you to run pipes down the road because the road runs alongside his property and he thinks the road belongs to him?'

'What sort of compensation?' said Julian.

'Full use of your electricity and water.' said Manuel.

'And of my body too?' I said.

Manuel explained that Croulard used to help himself to our services to do the work on his hamlet when our house was still in his family. Clearly our being there had pissed him off. I explained to Manuel that it was Croulard himself who told us about the treatment system Julian had then researched and we were about to install, and who had made a speech to us about how important it was to be environmentally friendly. He had stressed that when he built his complex of holiday homes he was going to have solar power and dry toilets. We had asked him if he wanted to share the system with us and he had said he did not want to share anything. And now he wanted free access to our electricity? Hadn't he also once said good fences make good neighbours? It was all too confusing.

'Why doesn't he just sell us that *petit bout*, that tiny square of land behind the house?' said Julian.

'You know,' said Manuel, 'asking someone from here to

sell or rent or lend you land, even a *petit bout*, is like asking them to tear a limb from their own body and give it to you.'

'When the mistral drops,' said Nadine, 'he will probably become more reasonable. Did you know that in old Napoleonic law, crimes of passion were excused if the wind had been blowing for more than three days? You have to watch him when the wind is up. Why not wait a while?'

'Why not ask Monsieur Chauvet if he wants your water?' said Manuel 'He has had that truffle orchard in front of your house for years but I do not believe he has had a single truffle because there is no water. Perhaps he could use it?'

Wasn't Chauvet the one, I thought, who, on our second meeting about the proposed system, had said, No thank you. Good boundaries make good friends?

'We've already suggested it to him,' said Julian. 'He's not interested.'

'But this year's truffle prices have reached record heights,' said Manuel. 'He could be a rich man.'

'Do you mean that if he took the free water we are offering him we would all have all free truffles?'

'I could grow my organic garden!' said Nadine.

'Or we could open a car wash' said Julian.

'Car wash with truffle café-concert?' I said.

It was time for the cheese platter. Nadine brought it in, and next to it she placed some rubbery orange squares. 'Quince jelly, made with the quinces you painted!'

Quince Half

ALICE'S STUDIO IS A PLACE OF ENCHANTMENT. In it, the grind of a south London suburb disappears in a puff of smoke, and we are transported into the Magician's cave, Santa's grotto or the Naughty Boy's bedroom. There are shells, wands and butterflies, swans, birdcages, aeroplanes, knitted cupcakes and dogs. There is a lavender radio on a stool, and on the tiny table at which Alice works there is just enough room for three china mugs full of pencils. There are drawings everywhere, and on the bulging bookshelves are five small paintings: Quince half obliterates the titles of the Book of Charms and the Book of Superstition, and leaning against a toy theatre on the top shelf are Apple half and walnut, Three cherries, Apple with a green bowl and Peony.

My studio is full of things which inspire or inform my work. In fact I am very selective about what I allow in here because it may come out in an illustration at a later date. I have never framed Julian's postcards because I like to see the edges, and pick them up from time to time, to hold them and examine the painting technique. Sometimes I rearrange them to make different relationships between them, and to see them in a fresh light.

Alice Wood, children's book illustrator and artist, London, UK

Still Life with Peeled Clementine

Gimme an O....! Gimme a B...! Gimme an A.....! I am
stuck in an office filling out tax forms, and I am going to
take today's clementine as the "O" for Obama I asked for
this morning on Facebook.

Jenna Nober, project manager, Chevy Chase, Maryland, USA

JULIAN IS A WILD FOOD LOVER. A man who, in an ideal
world, would like to concoct each of his meals from hedge-
rows, meadows, woods and rock-pools. In spring he might
prefer making elderflower champagne to painting cherries.
In summer, creating broom bud salad might lure him away
from the lavender fields. In autumn, when scarlet orchards
failed to inspire fiery landscapes in him, he might find himself
drawn to baskets piled high with mushrooms. (Cèpes, chanterelles, sheepsfoot, morels and the ragged bugles whose
name we couldn't figure out. Were they *trompettes de mort*
or *trompettes d'amour*? Trumpets of love or death?) Then
came winter. Although the mistral wind ensured that the
light was still good for landscape painting, it got very cold
and still life subjects were scarce. Chestnuts were small and
quinces were weird. Carrots, salsify and potatoes were boring
and there were only so many times you could paint a clementine. Clementine with blue tin. Clementine with candlestick.

Peeled clementine. Still life with blue mug and not another bloody clementine, thank you very much.

But sometimes clementines was all there was. Sometimes Julian would emerge from the Carpentras market with three plastic bags bumping into his thighs and biting into the fingers of one hand, almost pulling his shoulder out of joint with the weight of the tubers and root vegetables within. In the palm of his other hand he would carry aloft a single clementine with two perfectly angled leaves as if bearing a crown on a cushion.

The Truffle Orchard

For me, mushrooms are the forgotten force of nature. Everyone loves animals, even humans in some form. Everyone respects trees and flowers, for without them the world would be a very dull and hungry place. But without mushrooms we would live in an unfertile rubbish dump. It is fungus that breaks down all the detritus of other life. Even more importantly it is fungus who work underground and out of site to fertilize and nurture all plant life. Most of the world is too dry, at one time of year or another, to sustain plants without the fungi supplying them with water. Most of the land is too low in concentrations of trace elements and minerals without the efficiency of fungal plants finding and supplying them. Not only would we be very badly off for trees without fungi under the ground, we would not have the culinary delights of ceps. I love them flavored with paprika. Great colours together. Chanterelles are smashing with potatoes and truffles are perfect with eggs either in a jar together to flavor the eggs for an omelet or just thin slices on a plain fried egg to brighten a winter menu. Julian, please paint a truffle painting!

Roger Phillips, photographer and natural historian, London, UK

IT WAS EASY TO MISS the truffle market in Carpentras. This was not only because we had to get there early but because, when we were there, it merely looked like a few folk gathered outside a café to chat. However, once away from the rainbow bustle of the Friday stalls and up close, we could see that Something Important was going on. That Something Important concerned the 'black diamond of Provence' and it started at seven o'clock, in front of the Bar de l'Univers. There, unlabelled jars, each one with its lid screwed on tightly, were laid out in rows on four or five plastic-covered tables. Next to the jars were weighing scales, plastic bags and tongs. Behind the tables, men and women stood stiff and proud in sombre outfits. The tone was hushed and we trod respectfully. When we chose a jar, its lid was slowly unscrewed, and lifted just for a moment, and in that moment Julian stopped humming. He sniffed. He nodded. The lid was taken off completely. He picked out a truffle, weighed it in his hand, sniffed again and, as the aroma escaped briefly into the air, dreamed. Dreams of cauliflower and truffle soup, truffled eggs, drizzled truffle oil, truffle risotto, trout with truffles and truffle tagliatelle... When Julian nodded a second time the lid was hurriedly screwed back on, the dream extinguished (at least temporarily) and cash exchanged. The truffle was then wrapped and taken home to be stored in the egg box where it waited, gently infusing future omelettes.

To be honest, being so reverent toward something that looked like an oversized sheep-dropping made me giggle at first. That is until I smelled one. A wilder ingredient one could surely not find. Although they were expensive, they were no more so than meat or cheese, and one of them could transform the simplest ingredient into several meals fit for any gourmet. I too was hooked.

It was at about this time of year that Bernard, commenting on a clementine painting, wrote to say he was planning a visit. Luckily the black diamonds were still in season.

From: Bernard@withersanddraper.co.uk
Subject: bloody oranges

morning

I suppose that is a blood or seville orange, funny colour for an orange if you ask me (which I don't suppose you will). You know what'll happen don't you? You'll get famous and as soon as you get rid of your one-bar electric fire the muse will desert you, a bit like 'the Scottish play' bollocks. Of course it will ruin my image completely of the leisurely peintre doin' the south of france bit.

Anyway I like it... reminds me of your 1999 stuff I was so fond of. Not like all the fluffy stuff you are doing now. How are things going? I am planning a visit to the azure coast next week and thought I might drop in. B.

From: Jms@provenceart.fr
Subject: Fame

Ma Cher Bernardo,

Actually it's a clementine.

Things are going swimmingly. the wife spent most of the autumn in snobby, horsepooey, mozart cakey Salzburg, play-ing an opera Mozart wrote when he was 14. (think twinkle twin-kle little star but longer) but she's back now. Anyway she has dragged me kicking and screaming into the French tax system where, as it turns out, artists are treated like royalty. Being an artist here counts as a profession so I have the same social status as you but without the stigma and with tax breaks. You should get your watercolour set out and move here. Free advice from a professional. Shall I send directions? J.

From: Bernard@withersanddraper.co.uk
Subject: fluffy's directions

Nah, I'll find you. See you Tuesday around midday?

Tuesday came around. Julian found an uncluttered corner
of the temporary chipboard (soon to be granite, of course)
work surface, opened his favourite book, Roger Phillips'
Wild Food, on the mushroom page and set about preparing
lunch. He had just enough Italian durum wheat flour left
and so he decided to make his own pasta. Once chilled and
rolled out, he hung it in sheets over the kitchen chairs to dry.
Just before midday, he sliced the truffles, sliding his thinnest
sharpest knife into the moist grain. He set the slices aside
with a pot of crème fraîche. He floured the dry sheets of
pasta and curled them up carefully so they did not stick. He
cut them into ribbons, sprinkled them with flour one more
time, jiggled them around in a cloth to keep them separate,
and covered them. I refilled the pepper-pot and the parmesan
grater, set the table, and we waited. By two o'clock Bernard
had not called and by three, having abandoned the idea of
sharing our feast, we had eaten three portions of tagliatelle
with black diamonds.
At seven o'clock Bernard's email arrived.

From: Bernard@withersanddraper.co.uk
Subject: fluffy's house

I got as far as your village. Very nice too. Didn't know what to
do next so I turned round and went home. Pleasant drive. Next
year perhaps?

'But how long had he been driving?' I asked.
'He was coming from around Nice. Must have been
three hours each way.'

'What, and he didn't ask for directions when he got here?'

'No, apparently not.'

'And he didn't stop to phone you?'

'Neither did he display my self-portrait in his window like an escaped convict. Nope.'

'He's crazy! And he missed truffles.'

'He's just a guy. We don't ask. I would have done the same thing.'

Rougets - *Two Little Fish*

*Little Lisette, you are si belle with your belly d'argent and
your popper-snapper eye. I like you a lotte.*

Julia Gooding, soprano and cranio-sacral therapist, E.Sussex, UK

IT WAS CHRISTMAS EVE, and we were in Avignon's market,
Les Halles. Months before, Julian's inner ipod had scrolled
down to its Christmas playlist, and now the eighty-seventh
rendition of 'God rest you merry, gentlemen' was providing the background hum to our shopping. Julian was, he
said, preparing to cook for days. He was planning individual
stocks from gizzards, fowl necks, herbs, roots and wings
(*humty-tum*), that would find their way into sauces, terrines
(*hmm hmm*) and mousses. There would be tarts and nougats
glacés. First, however (*rumty tom - let nothing you dismay*),
we had to concentrate very hard. From one end to the other,
he insisted, we had to scour the fish stall (*tiddly pom*).

In front of us were langoustines, sea urchins, eels and
glow-in-the-dark starfish. There were tiger prawns and cock-
les, and coquilles St-Jacques. There were sole and whole
monkfish, squid and gilthead bream. The opulent display
glistened pink and silver.

'I would have the Utah Beach,' said the fishmonger as
our gaze hopped between Utah Beach, Gillardeau, Ile de Ré

and Ile d'Oléron oysters.

'I have been wanting to try the Gillardeau for years,' I said, 'everyone says they are the best.'

This year, still on a budget, Julian and I had set ourselves a challenge. This year we would only gift each other things that we could make. For my part this meant mastering Microsoft Excel and creating a filing system for Julian's chaos and clutter. For him, it meant making frames for our small collection of paintings. (Or, now I come to think of it, was that the year of the self-portrait? Or the compost bin? Either way, none were ever finished). It meant candles and a few carols. We would, however, permit ourselves to spend just that little bit extra on food.

'The Utah are as good as the Gillardeau,' said the fishmonger, 'and half the price.'

I hesitated. I always followed another's advice over and above my own instinct but was this my one chance in the year to try the oysters about which everyone raved?

'They're from a beach in Normandy, silly,' said Julian 'and not from a lake in Bryce Canyon.'

We chose the Utah Beach.

'I see you have now become truly Provençal in your tastes!' said the fishmonger as we added winkles and whelks that needed excavating from their shells with a two-pronged tool I, for one, had never glimpsed in an English cutlery drawer.

'Congratulations and happy holidays!'

It was time to move on to the fowl counter. The serving girl there was the daughter of our village butcher and, as we approached her, recognition turned into a wraparound smile that seemed to glitter under the tinsel trim of her red bonnet. We talked of where we would be spending the next few days, what the possibilities for snow and therefore sledging on the

Ventoux were, and of course we discussed what we would be eating. Then we asked her what the difference was between the posh Bresse and an ordinary free range capon. In a voice birdlike with excitement she answered. One was double the price, she said, and recommended we choose the other.

'Of course,' she added, 'I can deliver it tonight. In fact—' she waggled the neck of the creature like a ventriloquist—'I can deliver all your groceries direct to your door because I will be passing your hamlet on the way to visit my mother this evening, and it would be no trouble.'

'Thank you,' I said. 'One capon delivery to Les Couguieux later today would be much appreciated. Oh, and maybe the fish, too? That will allow us have lunch in town and I'm sure my husband will be happy about that.'

For the capon's vegetable accompaniments we chose cardoons, a distinctly unpaintable Provençal vegetable that looked like a cross between celery and a dinosaur, and tasted like a cross between celery and a Jerusalem artichoke. Then the even uglier salsify, a long thin root that sweated oily globules when you peeled it (which I found rather sexy) and roasted up as good as a parsnip.

'Excellent Provençal vegetables,' said the vegetable seller, stunned, I think, that an Englishman would know what cardoons were. We were starting to glow with the approval.

We queued for a loaf of country bread the size of a football and wandered over to the cheese stall. Piled high behind the glass were *picardons* and *pélardons*, crème fraîche and fromage frais, *fourme de* this and *coeur de* that, *bleus, briques, tommes* and *pavés*. And, of course, butter. Butter with grains of sea salt, unpasteurised butter, sweet unsalted butter, whipped butter and churned butter. Julian selected two kinds (*doux* for bread and sauces and *demi sel* for toast) and contemplated the goat's cheese. While he did so I found myself inspired to share with the waiting cheese man something of the delicacies we had savoured recently in Italy. Starting in Venice, I began by describing gooey mozzarella *di buffola* from our favourite shop on the lagoon. Then I moved on in my imagination to Verona and spoke about the *mostarda*, the pear conserve that was served with a selection of hard crystally sheep's cheeses. I was about to ask him if there was any such tradition of serving conserves with cheese in Provence when I realized the cheese seller was not listening. He had never been listening. In fact he had turned his back, started serving the next customer and left his assistant to issue our bill. I looked for Julian in the hope that he might be willing to bear witness to my memory, but he was not there.

I soon relocated my husband at the onion and garlic stall and we kissed. Much to his annoyance, however, it was not long before I was chatting again. This time I was enquiring about the difference between the pert pink garlic called Lautrec and the stripey, more baggy looking varieties. The garlic seller was telling me that the former was a hardneck variety and the latter a softneck. The Lautrec, he said as he caressed a bulb like he might the tear-streaked face of an upset child, was more refined. I asked him if it was true that most of that 'white' garlic we see in England or the States was from China where it was doused with chemicals to stop it sprouting, and grown in untreated sewage to blanch it. He said he thought that this information was correct. I thanked him and turned to Julian. Julian, however, was on the other side of the hall, standing in front of the potatoes.

Above the potato seller's display, season after season, year after year, there dangled a browning notice: *Manger les pommes de terre ça fait des beaux bébés.* Eating potatoes makes beautiful babies. Our dear potato seller was, unfortunately, far from beautiful. His head was as brown and misshapen as his produce, and his hair not unlike a cluster of roots sprung from it.

'It didn't work for my mother,' he said, seeing that I was looking back and forth between him and his sign. Then he beamed, showing a set of brilliant teeth that made me fall instantly in love with him.

'It didn't work for us either,' I said, '—yet. But we'll have a kilo anyway. You never know.' We all wished each other happy holidays and went back to the fishmonger to pick up our bags.

'Seeing this display always makes me think of Chardin,' said Julian, adding two silvery mackerel (affectionately called *lisettes*), a red snapper and a John Dory to our order. 'Just in case inspiration strikes!'

(I'm not sure how many perfect fish have expired in our fridge waiting to be painted, but that Christmas three certainly did.)

When we arrived home it was pitch dark. The mistral seemed to have laundered the sky, drawn down the Milky Way and augmented the moon, the light of which sketched a distant cherry orchard in black and chrome. The muscled limbs of a plane tree reached across the road, its fists clenched in protest at the cold. Vine stumps thrust their deformed fingers up from the freezing earth. The smells of liquorice, tobacco and roasting chestnuts filled the air. Shivering under the canopy of stars and hugging layers of fleeces to our skin, we listened to a medley of boar scuffles. Through the kitchen window, our Christmas preparations glowed in the firelight: Our 'tree', which consisted of a jug of tall twigs, stood on the table hung with baubles. Atop the tallest twig a cardboard angel covered in gold leaf perched precariously. At the base of the jug there sat an unruly wreath of holly.

We turned our key in the lock and dragged our bags inside. Once we had unpacked our groceries, our family-sized fridge bulged with decadence. One more winkle, I thought, and it might explode. We lit candles. We opened our oysters, our champagne and our carol books. We sat opposite each other and turned to 'In the bleak midwinter.'

'What can I give him...' we sang, I on the alto and Julian on the soprano line. A tear rolled down Julian's face. '...give my heart,' we sang in unison.

Flake White

Hello. I am interested in commissioning a small painting.
Perhaps lemons, garlic, or herbs. Or aubergines, purple like
cleric's robes? Something warm that will make me smile.

Imogen Davies, computer threat analyst, Brittany, France

WITH THE MONEY from her mother's estate Imogen
has big plans. Not only is she going to commission
her first painting but is, within the year, going to leave her
grown-up children and take a leap from southern England
to the French Atlantic coast, to a stone *longère* in Brittany.
She is going to replace dirt and concrete with ocean silvers
and sky greys, white clouds and black storms, and she has
chosen a particular artist to accompany her on the journey.
They have already agreed a price for two paintings. She is
so pleased that she writes again.

> The paintings will hang together over the fireplace in
> my dining room. The room is an organic room. It has
> sisal flooring, a cream hand-painted wooden table. The
> morning sun shines and falls upon the wall...

Suddenly Imogen feels a shiver of excitement at the thought
of colour, of bright hot pepper red.

> .. and if there is money over from the budget perhaps

you might do a tiny painting of a chili?

The reply from Julian the painter comes almost by return.

> Hi Imogen. I see something light in key, with inter-
> twined knots of garlic and an aubergine. Perhaps a
> black bottle or a cream jug. Some thyme, maybe, and
> a lemon. Very exciting. You had better check the width
> of your fireplace.

Imogen runs to find a tape measure. She opens every drawer,
chest and cupboard, she rummages among thimbles and
woolly socks but to no avail.

> Julian, no laughing please. I am five foot and I measured
> the width of the fireplace with my outstretched arms.
> It goes from the fingertips on my left side to my elbow
> on the right which, when I stretch one arm up and one
> arm down is the top of my head just past my derrière!
> So I am thinking, two foot six to be safe? If you like I
> will purchase a grown up measure.

Julian sends an image of two yellow quinces, a pink rose and
a blue cup as an example of what he imagines, and something about all that colour makes Imogen, at first, rather
nauseous. Then it makes her want to chat! She decides to
describe herself to her new friend. She says that she is a
Buddhist in training, and the last luddite in IT working for
a firm she calls The Monster, who wishes she could paint.
She says that to pass office hours she meditates cross-legged
and offers aromatherapy massage to stressed coworkers. She
adds that she has a maroon Ford Escort named Dante and
a PC named Pierre. There is so much more she wants to say.

Her senses are buzzing. She closes her eyes and tries to calm down. She imagines the white landscape to which she and her kids will be travelling in a week's time. Her breathing slows.

Christmas is a tough time for me so my kids and I are going to disappear to the Arctic circle. To eat ginger-bread in a log cabin. We will spend New Year's Eve with the Northern Lights. Happy Christmas to you both.

The break in Finland is good, very white. The Northern Lights dance like free spirits in a cold still sky like departed souls. Imogen and her daughter snuggle under reindeer furs and eat salmon pastries. They roll naked in the snow after saunas. Snow, snow, snow. White on white.

Soon after she returns, Imogen finds that Julian has launched a new website, and within a few weeks she has done something she could never have imagined doing. She has bought four bright red paintings! A chili pepper, a chili pepper and garlic, a pomegranate, and three clementines! Then, on the thirteenth of January, she opens up her email and sees her very own commissioned painting. Bluey black, pink and thyme green. She knows it is perfect for her Breton kitchen and she knows too, in that moment, that she will get there.

As the identical seasons shunt along in London, lots of red and purple things come and go in cyberspace. Figs and cherries and strawberries. Imogen keeps her colourful paint-ing wrapped in its box and takes it out occasionally to look at it. Meanwhile, Dante's head gasket blows and Julian's engine breaks. She sees Julian on the BBC sipping wine and then suddenly, in one day, he becomes famous. Apparently one mention in the New York Times has paid for the new engine in his car, and more. The emails from her new friend become short and grumpy and everything sells. This is all very well until she wants to buy another painting. She is jabbing at the link and it just won't come up. She refreshes the page, restarts Pierre, checks on another browser, tries touching the keys very gently whilst sending golden threads of compassion to the computer, and jabs again. She writes to the artist.

What a tease! Can't get to it!

Finally the page comes up and the painting she loves is sold. She can feel anger draining the flush from her face, and her fingers freeze on the keyboard briefly before she writes again.

I have unsubscribed. It's too frustrating. I sat here hitting refresh every two seconds and even then today's painting was sold before I had the chance to get to the web page. If you ever decide to give your pre-fame patrons a fighting chance to purchase new paintings please let me know. Otherwise, good luck.

Julian replies:

I am sorry, I made a mistake in the link, it is difficult as I cannot test it beforehand. Having said that... Well, hurtful is the word that comes to mind. I am not doing anything different.

The blade of anger stops twisting, and in its place there is grief. Pure as a snowdrift.

Dear Julian,
Hurtful? sorry, I didn't mean that at all. I will try and

explain.

Imogen explains that she is going to be 50 this year and that for forty-eight years she was a scruffy tomboy dreaming of the Amazon and trying to conform to other people's expectations, to live a life of ballet, baking and ribbons. Now, since her divorce, she has decided it is time to be HER.

Time to replace my depressed little life of monochrome anxieties with some fun and colour. You see, when I thought of my painting originally it was black and white. Slowly, in my imagination, I allowed for some pastel hues, but just a couple. A black aubergine, white garlic. It took a lot to let go and trust you to paint my painting as you imagined it and I was worried that it would be too much for me to appreciate and understand. So, it's not about accumulating art or following a fashion. It's about seeing the world through the eyes of someone who sees light and colour and beauty and learning that maybe I can too...

Two years later.

Imogen and Pierrick have been mussel hunting near the bay of Saint Brieuc and Imogen has returned home to study Finnish. She stands in the conservatory in what, only a year ago, was her new home. It has a sea-green dresser the length of the wall, and is full of plants. Light wood chairs have green-checked cushions and the floor is a deep terracotta. Above the fireplace is a long painting of garlic, an aubergine and a cream jug. To the right of the drinks table are five bright paintings that seem to glow in the sea-light. It is time, she thinks, to get back in touch with an old friend.

Dear Julian,

Remember me? I am now firmly ensconced in Brittany. I was going to say settled but we've had so many things go wrong, from broken toilets to electricity cuts, that 'settled' doesn't really seem appropriate. I'm starting to get used to the French way of working and setting my expectations accordingly (should I say lowering my expectations accordingly?). Anyway, I email to say that I am sitting here feeling cold and fed up in this unruly stone house, but that the sight of my paintings on the wall always makes me smile. so THANK YOU!!!

Every morning I look at Julian's postcards on our kitchen wall. My favourite one was from two weeks ago. garlic and a red hot chili, because I LOVE curry!

Iona Boyd, age 9, Leeds, UK

Single Malt

Just before the New Year, on the twenty-eighth of December, Julian painted a glass of whisky. It reminded me of a dear friend who now lives far away who greeted the dusk with a salute of single malt, neat.

Hope Schneider, partner in thought, La Canada, California, USA

JANUARY WAS ALWAYS A HARD TIME FOR JULIAN, and the first January at Les Couguieux, which we now discovered meant cuckoo hamlet and had nothing to do with mallow flowers at all, was perhaps the hardest. It was also the coldest and, with me back and forth from tour, the loneliest.

The painter, increasingly known locally, I imagined, as The Hermit, got up late with the lazy sun. He enclosed himself in a grubby designer bathrobe and said to himself, today I am going to paint. He passed his makeshift studio with an edge of excitement. Sometimes he stopped, opened the door, looked in and saw the easel standing with its back to him, like a gallows from which the blank face of a canvas stared out at the winter sky. Then he closed the door and descended to the kitchen. He made a fire in the grate and a bowl of porridge which he drowned in golden syrup. He added yesterday's cake of coffee grinds to the tower of coffee cakes on the chipboard surface, and pulled a fresh brew from the

machine. For a while he adjusted the marks on the wall that
indicated where he was, one day, going to build his fireplace.
He turned on his laptop, hovered his mouse over connect with
one hand and waited for the click, beep and warble of the
modem to start up. Usually he did not move from that spot
until he was hungry again, when he would get up to make
a baked potato or potato stacks with rosemary. This he ate
noisily making the fork screech on the plate. He licked the
plate clean, wiped his mouth on the sleeve of his robe, and
pushed the plate toward the other side of the table where
it clinked with his breakfast bowl. He pulled his computer
back toward him and fiddled some more with his HTML
until darkness extinguished yet another day.

I had known this obsessive state before and I had still not
forgiven Julian for its consequences. Two years previously
I had witnessed my beloved, hour after hour, day after day,
gambling away the profit from the sale of his London flat on
the stock market. In an attempt to what, I asked. Get rich?
Provide for us? Make sure he did not end up like his father,
a bank clerk struggling to feed five gaping mouths? Miss
out on the last potato ever again? But what about the fact
that his father had produced five happy children? And they
ten happy grandchildren? All of whom had enough potatoes. Didn't that count for riches? The concept of making
money out of money made me feel uncomfortable, but seeing
Julian pouring cash he had earned painting a lumpy lemon
or a bearded iris into the clutches of a doubtless environmentally disastrous company that didn't give a damn about
anything but the rocketing of their share prices broke my
heart. I knew deep down that to him, as it did to me, to be
rich meant to live a simple, meaningful and creative life, but
something else was driving him then and there was nothing
I could do but stand by and watch. The memory was still

vivid between us as I watched him now. It did not occur to me that this time Julian might be building something rather than destroying everything.

'I've got a hunch......' Julian said, not taking his eyes of the computer screen. Though I was now home, he didn't seem to have changed his routine much. '..that a post every day about the light of Provence, the changing seasons, the painting process and perhaps even what we are eating for dinner, might... ' He trailed off.

The rain thumped the window panes. I didn't care to know about new websites. I just wanted Julian to bloody do what he was good at doing. Paint.

Julian resumed. 'There's this new phenomenon called blogging. I am trying to create a website which would take the form of a studio diary, you see. Do you see?'

I cleared away the tower of coffee cakes and threw Julian's bathrobe in the wash. Julian, now in my bathrobe, stayed glued to his computer.

'I am following daily web postings,' he said 'and working with this new thing called moveable type to...'

I dropped a much loved Garland cup into the washing up bowl and chipped a handle. Julian did not budge. I washed up loudly.

'I'm not sure about the domain name,' Julian called over my din. 'Or the font. It has to be exquisite, of course. No good having paintings if you haven't got a gallery in which to show them, and a beautiful website with a beautiful font is like a gallery and an agent all rolled in to one.'

I slapped a cloth on the work surface. Still bloody chipboard, I thought.

'Come over here,' said Julian, opening his towelling-covered arms wide, 'and stop being so smelly. Can't you just relax and trust me?'

Obviously I couldn't.

'Anyway,' continued Julian, 'I want to show you my final type selection.'

Reluctantly I pulled up a chair next to my husband and looked at the screen. On it was a cream oblong in which the words Permanent Red were written. In his 'lightbox', Julian explained, sat Goo goo gjoob, EF Petroglyph, Helvetica, Tully Bold, Gauguin, Giggle script, Cézanne, Vincent and Baka Too. The most obvious choice with which to start seemed, he said, to be Cézanne.

He pulled the example up. I could almost hear the scratching of the artist's nib and yet the script was so fragile that it pained me to witness the sentence 'Battle frizz with quick hair epoxy gel' written in it. Julian switched to the alternative: 'Jackdaws love my big sphinx of quartz.'

'You see the way the t is crossed?' he said. 'That is the sort of perfect mark I long to make, and yet perhaps it is the sort of mark that only the son of a banker who has no need to earn his living can afford. Unlike Van Gogh, you see, Cézanne didn't need to be understood. He just needed to paint, to follow his vision.'

'And if you didn't need to earn a living,' I said, 'would you paint?'

'No, I would laze about, learn the piano, travel to Singapore and eat soft shell crab. I am not like Cézanne, or Guillamon who won the pools and just kept right on going. I only paint because I can, because I always could. Because I never understood why other boys couldn't, and if I have to earn a living, it beats a nine-to-five.'

Once Julian had registered a password, the website allowed him to sample any combination of words in the script of his choice so we decided he would try out his own name in his hero's writing. As soon as he saw it, however, Julian moved respectfully on to another hand. Gauguin was next up. Jackdaws love my big sphinx of quartz, wrote Gaugin. His writing made me think of my grandmother's shopping lists, all slim back-hand and neat double loops, but with an occasional curly d swooping back to kiss the previous letter in a burst of creativity. I noticed that, although all the letters were usually joined, the letters of the word love were not. Julian moved through Goo goo gjoob, Giggle, Tully Bold and Vincent. Then he arrived at Helvetica.

'You see,' he said. 'No information. Just a neutral space for the image and the imagination.' Julian closed the laptop. 'Helvetica it is.'

After the Rain

..And then Julian built Shifting Light. It was like witness-
ing a rocket on the launch pad—kind of exciting and a
little nerve-racking. Some worried thoughts went through
my mind. Will it work—is it the right thing to do—should
Julian paint a painting a day—what would Cézanne think?
With fingers crossed we watched Julian take off.

James Roberts, media producer, Sydney, Australia

BEFORE WE LEFT FOR THE STATION the next day, Julian and I took our morning walk at the foot of the mountain. As usual, to avoid being followed by Oscar, we had to leave separately and we had to jog. I ran down to the bottom of the road first and, hiding behind an oak tree, watched Julian bob toward me. He seemed to be moving more from left to right than forward and occasionally he kicked one leg high in the air and grinned. His curls, jutting out at a right angle to his ears, moved up and down independently of his cranium like separate limbs, and his arms flapped in the air about waist height as if he were trying to take off.

'So', he said, puffed out on arrival. 'What about this domain name? Permanent Red isn't quite right. Too angry. What about Mr Fluffy's painting by numbers?'

Like so many paintings with whose beginnings I had

fallen in love and whose completion I was unlikely ever to see, I felt the need to protect myself from getting too involved in the new Web project. Yet, in this state of childlike wonder, Julian was hard to resist.

'What is Permanent Red anyway?' I asked.

'An artist's pigment and book by John Berger about seeing that changed my life.'

I could hear Oscar crying out his abandonment at the top of the road.

'What about An English Artist in Provence?'

'Sounds like a song by Sting. It's got to have something about the light...'

'Painter's Light... ?'

'Or the seasons. And changing... '

'Painted Light, Moving... Shifting... Mr Grumpy's Landscapes... Seasons. Shitting, I mean Shifting Provençal Seasons?'

A posse of lozenge-shaped clouds slid across the top of the Ventoux.

'Mr Berger's Cloudscapes? Mr Badger's Permanent Cloudscapes?' I said. ' ...Shifting Light?'

There was a silence.

'Shifting Light,' he said. 'Yes. I like it.'

Cloud Shadows

*Julian confirms that painting is like running, or the violin,
or the cello...it requires practice, all the time. I am so sick
of the people who think it pours out like a leaky tap, like
it is easy, or god given.*

Sarah Wimperis, artist and illustrator, Cornwall, UK

I WAS AWAY ON TOUR AGAIN. Though the opera provided a
sturdy scaffold for my evenings, the rest of my time was
falling apart. At night, too much information was being
exchanged, skin was being drawn to skin and affairs were
springing up everywhere in the orchestra. I clung to my
marriage but sometimes it felt like a ghost in a gaudy dressing
room. Before each performance, I phoned home and talked
into the void. I said that someone who waggled her hair a
lot had been writing love notes to the conductor. I read the
menu from a Japanese restaurant I had found, or described
a dire curry I had had. I'm working, Julian said. Or: you're
talking AT me. At least pause occasionally so I can breathe.
Sometimes he said how cold he was, and I tried not to ask
him how much wine he'd consumed. We said we loved each
other, agreed to talk again in the morning and hung up.

One night I called late and Julian sounded weird, like
he had been crying. I had taken a half-bottle of Bordeaux

from the minibar, rinsed the coca cola cup in which I had been keeping my toothbrush and poured the wine in to it. I placed the cup on the bed and dialled.

'How has your day been, my love?'

'I fiddled on the computer a bit. I don't really want to talk. You know I'm not very good on the phone and I'm watching a film.'

'I just wanted to tell you about the concert. It was good, I think. I was watching Jean-Marie warm up backstage beforehand. He was whizzing around in seventh position like a Russian virtuoso when he really only needs to go as far as second for this music. Meanwhile Yuri and I were back to back doing our meditation on open strings—you know that thing when I do those long slow bows and sync it up to my breathing? Well he does the same thing, it turns out and... '

I opened my laptop and looked at my screen-saver. It was a picture of Julian in his Renoir tee shirt beaming straight at me. A field of lavender arched behind him and his manicured fingers rested on an easel.

'Darling, I don't really want to talk,' he said. 'I'm depressed. I just need you to be here.'

'But it's no different when I am there,' I said. I tugged at a threadbare blanket.

'That's because I know you are going away again.'

The pause timed out on Julian's movie and I could hear a voice talking about baseball. I tried another tack:

'I'm reading this fantastic book about living in the present... '

'But I'm watching a film.'

'OK.'

'You know, I just want you to come home.'

I rested my free elbow on the kidney-shaped side table. The turquoise plastic clashed with the meadowsweet green sweater Julian had bought me in Skye.

'I'm going now,' said Julian.

I hung up the phone when I heard the dialling tone. I stared out of my hotel window at the advert for Calvin Klein underwear glowing in the streetlight. The life-sized stud with his bulging Y-fronts at eye level looked straight back at me. I pulled my coat around me and went to the bar to join Yuri. That was the night everything changed.

Night Lemon

I have been a manuscript editor, mostly for academic publishers, for twenty-five years. I loved what the job used to require (the red pencils, the layers of editorial shorthand on well-thumbed pages, collegial debate over grammar and usage) and did not require (electricity, for one thing). I married a printer, partly, I think, because he too loved the smell of paper and ink. The Internet changed all that, for better and worse.

For better: the Internet made it possible to live anywhere and still conduct business as usual—in my case, that meant my husband and I could move from San Diego to a beautiful small town in central Virginia and I could work from a dedicated home office filled with music, my child's artwork, and, frequently, her voice. No commute equals saner pace of life (with obvious ethical/environmental benefits). The Internet also made in-depth research possible without proximity to a major university library.

For worse: academic publishers soon realized they didn't need big in-house editorial staffs, and legions of capable, irreverent, experienced book editors were cut loose to fend for themselves as independent contractors. Gone the lovely sense of collaboration, the sessions of semantic parsing over coffee in someone's office. Also gone, the tactile pleasures of editing and book making, since much manuscript transmission and manipulation is now electronic. The business part of the business is also more impersonal and more hurried. Corners are cut. At some point, I realized I'd been working for one client for three years without ever hearing his voice—now I make at least a couple of phone calls, if only for mutual introductions, for new projects. You do what you can to keep something human, and handmade, in the process.

Which brings me to Postcard from Provence. In 2002 I began collecting interesting images I came across on the Internet in an idiosyncratic electronic archive. At first black-and-white photography, then other kinds of original artwork as the amount of material posted online mushroomed. I can't always explain why an image is qualified to be in my archive, just as I can't always explain why one sentence works and another doesn't, except to say that it must be good. (I get to define good—it's immensely satisfying.) One day early in 2005 I image-googled something—lemons, just because there was a bowl of lemons in front of me—and among many hits, this caught my attention: Three Lemons. Curious, I kept looking and ended up at Julian's site.

Whenever I resent the Internet for the editorial impersonality and disconnection I've experienced, I remind myself that connects me to good people and good work, handmade, still.

Viqi Wagner, book editor, Midlothian, Virginia, USA

B UILD IT AND HE WILL COME,' said Julian.
His voice on the phone had, in twenty-four hours, gone from sounding like coffee dregs to whipped egg whites. I could tell that when he finished watching Field of Dreams

the night before, something had broken free in him.

'That's what I'm going to do, Oscar. Ruth. Manon. Good King Wenceslas. Whoever. I'm going to build it, and they are going to come... '

'Sounds great,' I said, still somewhat weary. 'What else is new? Any exciting Bedoin gossip or post?'

'Just a card from your Mum and another bloody France Telecom bill. And I saw an orchid.'

'Better open it, I guess. The bill not the orchid.'

Though he did not speak well, Julian's understanding of French was decent. That was partly due to five years watching dubbed Agatha Christie movies. Today, however, as he opened the letter, I could hear that that this was a moment in which he did not trust that understanding one bit.

'They must be bloody kidding!' he said in high pitch as if the egg-whites in his voice were stiffening and peaking. 'Living at the bottom of a mountain with no mains drainage... '

As always, I feared the worst.

'I'm just double-checking the address to see it's not some horrible trick.'

Julian read the letter out loud and I listened.

'A.D.S.L.,' he said. 'That stands for Asymmetric Digital Subscriber Line. Must be universal, no?'

'Internet is the same word in French. Access too, pretty much, give or take an accent... '

'And *haut débit* has, surely, to mean high speed?'

'Or: you owe us a whole lot... '

'It cannot be true.'

'No, it can't. We've only just got an electricity supply out there. It must be a mix up with our old address in Crillon, surely?'

The repercussions of this for a hermit could be enormous,

we agreed. First of all, there would be Radio Four on tap. There would be Just a Minute and The Archers, The Food Programme, Desert Island Discs, Book at Bedtime... (I was sure Julian was spinning round in the kitchen at the prospect of being reunited with all these old friends.) The game of Pass the Cable would be no more. There was The Guardian on line, ordering art materials on line, Italian designer taps and sausages, cat food and thermal underwear on line. The Mac Shop on line. In the future, of course, there would be downloadable TV, movies and music. All with one screen and no cables. The world would not just be on our doorstep, it would be inside our living room. In fact Julian would never have to deal with the outside world again.

'I think it is true,' he said. 'Broadband has come to Les Couguieux!'

'No!' I said.

'Yes! And one thing is certain—building it will be a whole lot easier from now on. I'm going to the studio right now. I feel a night lemon coming on.'

Espresso and Silver Spoon

From these two 'Internet painters,' Julian and Duane, the spider web of discovery weaves, the connections ping and spin from one painter to the next, Australians even, demonstrating with absolute clarity why we call the Internet the web.

James Roberts, media producer, Sydney, Australia

WITH HIS NEW-FOUND FREEDOM, Julian started researching. Feverishly. The great expanse that was cyberspace was, at that time, he said, mostly full of site developers and geeks. There were a few minimal photo sites that caught his eye. There was a guy called Dean Allen who posted a cool picture every day of his two Weimaraner dogs sitting, running, eating, farting, whateverring, and the photographs received visitors in their thousands. There were also a few artists. There were things called blogs: cool blogs, teen blogs, webby blogs, catty blogs and rude blogs. And then there was Duane Keiser.

'Check him out,' Julian said, already sounding intimate with the artist whom he had found on Boing Boing. 'He's incredible!'

A painter and professor in Virginia, Keiser did a post-card-sized painting every day. He posted them on a basic dot blogspot site, and they were selling. Every one was selling.

'Look at today's!' said Julian. 'Look at this peanut butter and jelly sandwich. It's brilliant! He's brilliant!'

This, from someone who scolded me for using so many superlatives.

'No gallery. No middleman. A hundred dollars a day three hundred and sixty-five days a year...well, let's say three hundred with weekends and holidays. Do the math, as they say...'

He paused to calculate.

'That's thirty thousand dollars a year! That's double what I got as manager of the cinema in London! I could do that! I can paint small paintings! I have always painted small paintings! I don't have to paint houses covered in snow, or irises in winter. I could earn thirty thousand a year, darling, and paint what's on the doorstep, and you wouldn't have to keep going away. You could live here with me, my love, all the time! In glorious Provence!'

It was normally me who phoned while I was on tour, but the next day Julian called again. And the next, and for the rest of the week we gathered around our macs every morning, him on his brand new ADSL and me on the Ibis hotel's WiFi.

'I would kill for that series of egg yolks. Did you see them?' Julian said.

'And a lovely chocolate covered cherry today.' I looked at the screen. Then down at my hotel coffee. It had skin.

'But did you see the seedpod he did last Wednesday?'

'Delicious.' I sliced an apple into a bowl and stirred in some Danone fat-free yoghurt. I was counting the days until my return in yoghurt pots and I saw that this was pot number twenty of twenty-one. 'The last Rameau tonight...'

And the little espresso cup? Telephone pole in a fog?'

I could hear Julian steaming the milk. I could do with a proper cup of coffee, I thought.

'Yes. It sold within minutes, didn't it? It was very dinky.'

I could tell that he wanted to get off the phone so he could continue the work on his website but he couldn't stop talking either.

'I'm excited!' he said. 'I'm tingly all over! The tingles are going down my forearms, across my ribs. Unless I'm having a heart attack. Just kidding. I think I'm in love. Mostly with myself of course. It's as if a light has gone on. I'm going to start today!'

'Start what?' I said.

It was then that then the man who never, well, rarely painted said:

'I'm going to start doing a painting a day.'

Oyster Shell and Cup

Julian and Duane's paintings hang side by side like a couple of buddies: Duane's blue marbles next to Julian's orange Clementines.

James Roberts, media producer, Sydney, Australia

I TOOK A TABLE IN THE BAR LA MARINE and, resisting the pricey Gillardeau oysters, ordered a plate of '*Fines de claires d'Oléron*'. From the train I had run straight to the port where I picked the bluest café with the most boat paraphernalia. I spread the nautical napkin on my lap and reached for the butter in its little brown pot. I scraped the dewy surface with a knife and slathered my rye bread with calories. Behind me the town of La Rochelle glowed softly, rounded by the sea breeze like a pebble. Its arched streets curled like caterpillars. Its shutters were grey as the sky, and its stone white as a cloud. Sails flapped in the wind and the aluminum of boat masts tinkled in the pale air. This was the day when Postcard from Provence went live. With an oyster. And, because of a single manila envelope that got away, I was not home to celebrate.

A couple of months previously I had been making up a bunch of CVs. However, when Julian saw the plain white typing paper emerging from the printer with its florid list of dates and degrees in Lucida Chancery he shrieked. 'Oh God! You can't send your CV looking like that! First of all I need to design you a header, and then you have to space it properly, and—Christ, no! Not that font. It has to be something classic.'

'Like Helvetica?' I asked.

'Yes. Like Helvetica. You have no idea how much this stuff influences people.'

'But, darling, it's just a CV. I've been sending them out for years. Look, I'm not a soloist in need of a swanky brochure. French orchestras, just like any other orchestras, want to know when you're born and what you've done. That's all. They get loads of them every day.'

'That's exactly why yours has to be special. It has to stand out and be a thing of beauty'.

'But I like the italic look…'

My words trailed off. I knew he was right. I picked up the one envelope that had already been stamped and addressed to Lyon and put it in my pocket ready to post later in the day. The exquisite CV never got made, of course, but I did send the single manila envelope, and these oysters, in this port, on this tour, with one of the top period instrument orchestras in France, were the result.

'You really should try the Gillardeau,' said the waiter, bringing my wine. I was smiling at the memory of Julian and his fonts, but I wasn't falling for the waiter's charm. I reiterated my order of the *Fines de claires*. When they arrived I sat and looked at them, thinking about a certain painting that had just appeared on the Web. Their obstinate feet were cut. I brought one up to my nose and sniffed the sea. Then I brought it down to my mouth. As my teeth grazed it, releasing its sweetness, my mobile rang.

'Sold it!' said Julian. 'I've sold the oyster! The first

Postcard from Provence is off to Poughkeepsie! And the same guy wants to buy the chilies I did last week!'

'That's wonderful,' I said and beckoned the waiter. 'Monsieur: and six Gillardeau, if you please!'

'And you'll never guess what! Duane has offered to swap his seedpod with my sun, wind and rain!'

Mozart Letters and Daisy

*I like small things, small containers, and Julian's paintings
remind me of songs by Mozart: small containers filled
with big ideas and emotions. I adore still lifes generally,
despite the whole vanitas thing; that era of Dutch paintings, the moment when daily life permeated art. Maybe
it's because I'm on tour so often and so often homeless... .*

Lisa Saffer, soprano, Brownfield, Maine, USA

S USANNA...,' SANG FIGARO. And again, preceded by that
heart-wrenching O. Down below, as the continuo player
in the pit, I caressed the gut of my string and descended the
arpeggio, following the motion of Figaro's body as he fell
to his knees.

When the curtain came down for the end of the first act
we trotted to our dressing rooms. In the odorous oblong of
the ladies' a selection of snacks were being handed round.
Dried mango slices, bran biscuits, and cake left over from a
child's birthday party. Tea was being poured from an urn into
polystyrene cups about whose environmental impact many
of my colleagues were unhappy. String players were laying
out packets in readiness for the next tour. Quick change:
Mozart to Puccini, gut to steel, flat shoes to high heels, A415
- A440. Dlugolecki to D'Addario. As reverence for the music

turned to the usual chatter about kids with temperatures and motorway jams, and lipstick and deodorant were reapplied I switched on my palm. I went to my Facebook page and searched for our Figaro. There he was with his thousand and two friends. I prodded the keyboard and wrote: Bravo for Sunday Peter! Your lines for tonight are spaghettini, peperoncino, fagiolini and, because it is the last night… '

So far, at my insistence, Peter had managed to slip three extra words effortlessly in to each performance of The Marriage of Figaro. Tonight, however, he was going to get a shock. I typed in a fourth ingredient and pressed return.

Then I typed 'shiftinglight' into my browser. There was the day's painting and there, as if they had walked straight out of the wings and on to the stage to sing a trio, were three of my shoes. One concert shoe, one wedding slipper and one bright orange, curly-toed moccasin. Under the painting Paul had written: Lovely! Which pair do you wear when you're out plein air painting?

I chuckled and returned to the pit for the second half of the opera. Ninety minutes later Peter ran off stage with Susanna singing spaghettini, peperoncino, fagiolini and vindaloo. The curtain fell, and rose again. The dancers at the front of the stage folded from the waist and their lanky arms flopped onto their toes. I took my bow, shoving my bottom out into the viola section and craning my neck to watch the clapping. Then I sat down. I looked around at the faces of my fellow musicians. Tomorrow, I thought, this tour will finally be over and I will be on a train going home to Provence. To Julian and his postcards, and to shifting light. It was the first time in many months, I realized, that I couldn't wait. I took my final bow and skipped out of the pit.

Boats at Amalfi

For several years we travelled to Hyeres for the cane festival in June. This year, however, our daughter is expecting her first child around that time so we cannot go. Perhaps, Ruth, we are not destined to meet, but only know each other through our passion for a painter and his work...

Janet D'Addario, graphic artist, Old Westbury, New York, USA

NEW YORK HARBOUR, 1905. Carmine D'Addario, a young lad of 14, stands at the rail of an ocean liner, his wool coat wrapped tightly around his throat against the wind and drizzle. The trip from Naples has been long, cold, and rough. Someone shouts. A murmur runs through the crowd as they peer through the fog and salt spray. Suddenly, in the distance, a pinpoint of light, then a looming figure emerges from the mist. More shouts. Before them stands Lady Liberty, raising her flame against hard times, guiding them into New York City. People cheer at the sight of her, reaching their hands out in gratitude. As tears of joy mix with the rain on his cheeks, Carmine—or Charles, as he will soon become known—stares at the statue on Ellis Island and thinks, I want her to watch over me.

Together with thousands of other European immigrants seeking fame and fortune in America, Charles D'Addario sets up home just a few miles from Liberty, in Astoria, Queens. There, with his brother-in-law Rocco, he starts up his business as a string maker. The pavements are not lined with gold. It is grueling work and Rocco returns home to Italy, but Charles succeeds. By 1918, he has begun manufacturing strings in the tiny garage behind his home. It will not be long before he is providing every kind of string to some of the most celebrated clients in the world, at the dawn of the Jazz Age.

Fast forward a century. We are on a well-to-do residential street in Nassau County, just off the Long Island Expressway, in between a country club and the State University of New York. Nearby are Ben's Kosher Deli, the Zen Palate, and Benny's Ristorante. This is Janet's story.

'About a decade ago, my husband Jim and I took a trip to Salle, a little coastal town near Pescara, where Jim's grandfather, Charles D'Addario, was from. Jim's ancestors were shepherds during the summer months, and when it came time to slaughter the sheep, they managed to sell off everything but the intestines. Many members of the family must have been players of the lute or early guitar and quickly the D'Addarios realized that these resilient parts of the animal were ideal for making the gut strings they needed to replace so frequently. As early as 1680 one of the D'Addario family gravestones in Salle describes the deceased as a *cordaro*, or string maker. Soon, the D'Addarios' hand-made strings were being traded across Italy, the home of the world's finest violin makers. But in 1905, Salle was devastated by an earthquake and young Charles, and his brother in law Rocco, decided to head to America to continue the family string business there. They set up in Astoria, Queens, where many other ex-Salle immigrants now lived. Today, his direct descendants,

still in New York, run the largest musical string company in
the world, making over 600,000 strings every day.'

Janet pauses to take a breath.

'By now, Ruth,' she says, 'you must be asking... '

'Yes, I am,' I say. 'What has this to do with Provence
and Julian?'

Janet's answer is unexpected, and at first puzzling.

'Well,' she says, 'we also make reeds.'

'Reeds for clarinets and oboes kind of reeds?'

'Have you heard of Rico Reeds?'

Here's the other part of Janet's story.

May 1893. The 'Belgravia' docks at Ellis Island and begins
unloading its cargo of over thirteen hundred immigrants.
Among them are two brothers in their late teens who have
run away from seminary school near Naples. Clutched in
their hands they have four small cases, each of which guards a
musical instrument: a guitar, a harp, a mandolin and a violin.

Libereto and Joseph Rico work hard, establishing themselves as respected musicians in New York and Chicago.
Music flourishes in the family and Libereto has a son, Frank,
who becomes a clarinettist with the Walt Disney studios.
There, in Los Angeles, Libereto finds that good clarinet reeds
are in short supply and he begs his uncle Joseph, now an
established composer living in Paris, to help out. That is
how, in 1928, from his holiday home in the Var region of
southern France, Joseph Rico sends the first shipment of 350
kilos of reed cane to California, thus becoming the founder
member of the company on whose reeds the world's greatest jazz tunes are still played.

Janet concludes:

'From their humble origins in those two boats bound

from the bottom of the Amalfi coast to Ellis Island, Rico Reeds and D'Addario strings are now in partnership. And now I am going to tell you what this has to do with Julian! This is why, every year in June, we go to Provence, to the cane festival in Hyères. There we see the magical grasses that have been harvested and de-husked, and are drying in the sun ready to make into our clarinet reeds. There, in 2003, we saw the launch of a posthumous album of Joseph Rico's waltzes and serenades, and there we hope, next year, to meet the painter of the postcard paintings we collect...

..And by the way,' adds Janet, giving a quick glance at her computer screen, 'right now, as you can imagine, I've got my eye on Boats at Amalfi.'

Lemon

I have a friend who lives on a hill and has raised a Meyer lemon tree. It is a small tree that produces not a lot of lemons but they are very good, somewhat sweet lemons. Every time I visit him, he lets me pick a lemon to take home. Now I live in Germany and he in San Francisco and I don't get to visit very often. I miss the lemon tree and my friend. Months ago, Julian painted a lovely picture with a lemon in front of a blue box. The yellow against the aqua was perfect. I saved it as my computer background so every day I can think about lemons and friends.

Kat Glans, graphic designer, Stuttgart, Germany

IN THE FLURRY of last-minute dinner preparations, Julian poured himself another glass of wine. Our guests that night were professional chefs and I could tell by the fragmented nature of his humming that Julian was a little nervous. As always, the house was in chaos. The kitchen table was covered in cat prints and coffee rings and in the corner of the room the naked bricks of half an open fire were in need of plaster. Meanwhile the stove top looked not like a cook's haven but like a science experiment. We had been making paint at home, using ammonium, fromage blanc, melted beeswax, vodka, *terre verte* and *noir fumé* pigments, and the 'happy marriage, traditionally used to paint troikas' of which the book boasted, had become a malodorous mess. Julian, in search of some condiment or other, was trying to free his hand from between the flat stomach tea-bags and the anti-hairball cat food when the computer pinged.

'A lawyer in Boston wants to buy my lemons!' he said. 'And hang on, he says he is a friend of Jo and George!'

'Quelle surprise,' wrote Julian with one duck fat–covered finger. 'Your friends are just about to arrive for dinner and the exact lemon in your picture is about to become a lemon surprise pudding for them! I'll pack it and send it off as soon as it's dry. Probably in about ten days' time. J.' The man in Boston sent back a line in which he said something about it being a small world and wished us all bon appetit.

Jo and George arrived. We ate pheasant and potato gratin as I recall. Then we ate cheese, and opened the fourth bottle of wine just about the time a toad arrived to warn us about the coming downpour. We watched the creature pulsing in the cat flap. We talked some more, as we always did, about food. Suddenly Julian got up, tottered a bit on his feet and announced that it was time to construct the pudding.

It was unusual for Julian to try a recipe he didn't know, especially for the cooks we admired most in the world. He preheated the oven, cracked, whisked, squeezed, folded and sieved. He hummed, of course, and drank some more. We continued talking.

'One grain. One vegetable,' said Jo, dreamily.

'No square plates,' I said.

'Or slate ones,' said Julian.

'No fucking bullshit,' said George.

'And Great Coffee,' I said.

'That moment when you cross the border and that first service station with its Illy dispenser and its handsome waiters who know not to pull too hard,' said Jo.

'I bet that's not what the local girls say,' said George.

'Georgio,' said Jo, nudging him under the table with her calf, bare now that she had slid her legs out of her woollen tights for comfort.

'And the coffee in Spain!' I said.

'Now, of course, poor France is all wrapped up by *bon...*' said Jo.

'...Or *mauvais* as we call it,' said George.

'Yes,' I said, 'bad café. Buy the coffee get the machine free. What is a poor struggling bar owner to do? And what did you think of Nespresso, George?'

'Well if it's good enough for George Clooney,' said Jo. 'By the way, love the new site. It's like getting a little post-card from Provence every day.'

'Nespresso is the worst coffee I ever had in my life,' I said, 'and besides, it is an environmental disaster with all those little capsules and fancy boxes.'

'Julian,' said Jo, 'we have a friend staying next week. Donna Paul. She is a journalist and photographer. She has an impeccable and discerning eye. She has seen our collection of your paintings and we want her to see more. We thought... '

'Best coffee I ever had,' said George. 'We now serve only Nespresso in the restaurant. It's totally reliable. Never a dud.'

'Did you hear what Jo said, Julian? About a postcard from Provence?'

Julian got up and was moving toward the oven. I noticed he was swaying on his feet and I feared for the lemon dessert.

'I propose a toast to my favourite restaurant in the Vaucluse!' said Jo, standing up. 'To chez Julian!'

Julian took the dessert out of the oven. It hissed a bit, caved in and died.

'Sorry,' said Julian after George had tried, and failed,

to rescue it. 'Chef's a bit pissed tonight. Surprise hic Lemon Still Life Pudding chez Julian is off.'

Apple and Goat's Cheese

*I had discovered that I was lactose intolerant, I remember.
The sticky film of residue dairy products left behind was
becoming unbearable, so I made a simple life change. I
cut milk out of my life. It was then that I found another
life-drink, akin to nectar, sweet, tart, and and cleansing. It
was then that I discovered Julian and decided I was ready
to return to oil painting.*

Linda McCann, Knoxville, Tennessee, USA

MARKET DAY IN BEDOIN is on Monday, and my new job
was not only to get the week's shopping, but to find
postcard-sized things to paint. It was easier in winter when
all the lavender-scented cicada-shaped garlic-crusher stalls
had disappeared, and we were left with the bare bones: the
misshapen vegetable sellers, the cane basket maker (who,
even though his basket had seen me through several Provençal winters, still wished me happy holidays), the florist, the
beekeeper and his honey-maker wife and, best of all, the
Goat Lady.

The Goat Lady, genuinely goateed, greenish and angular
like her herd, was not a pretty sight. However, her cheeses,
subtly perfumed, sprigged with thyme, winter savory or lavender, and rounded by hand, were beautiful. I would mix

the creamy ones with herbs, serve the thimble-shaped ones called *bouche-trous* ('gobstoppers') with an aperitif, and toss the drier *crottins* ('little shits') in with roasted beetroot and hazelnuts. Julian loved to paint the high-sided *pélardons*. Her cheeses could stuff vegetables, make desserts, be crumbled on top of a gratin, enhance a soufflé or run all over your cheese board like a naughty brie. They were easy to digest and utterly delicious. Every Monday we, along, I suspected, with everyone in the surrounding villages, looked forward to them, and indeed the gruff, goatish smile we would receive when the Goat Lady handed them over. In fact every Monday, when I saw her lips part to reveal that row of small, sharp incisors, I was so overcome with gratitude that I made the same promise to myself: that I would bring her a copy of the *pélardon* Julian had painted. And every Monday I forgot, until one Monday it was too late. One Monday the Goat Lady was gone.

The Relais du Ventoux was the place, I decided, where I might find clues to my favourite cheese-maker's whereabouts. With its plastic chairs laid out on uneven paving in front of the school, the café was always full. There, teachers, potters, mushroom pickers and mothers, dustbin-men and policemen, bow makers and dope smokers exchanged the week's gossip over a pastis, coffee or *menthe à l'eau*. I took a table in the sun, put down my *pélardon*-less load of painting subjects and listened. Some of the talk around me was about the fact that the village wanted to make the central parking area back into a square with the possibility for a boules piste. Women were haughtily exchanging recipes. ('A dob of butter' or 'A pinch of pepper' or 'A spoonful of crème fraîche, and your dish will be transformed.') There was news that a man had been shot accidentally by a hunter at dusk, that another had been out poaching truffles and had not been seen since, and that there was going to be a new farmers' market on the road to Flassan. And then there was this.

'It's because of EEC regulations.'

I knew immediately about whom the woman with the teacup cheekbones was talking.

'But have you seen her goats?' said another whose several chins were swaddled in a polo neck sweater. 'I went to buy cheese directly from her farm once, and hers were the most immaculate three goats I have ever seen. She fed each one of them a separate diet, you know, from three separate fields. The one that produced the milk that made the cheese with the thyme on top she kept in a pasture with thyme. The same with the savory and the lavender, which is why the sprig on the top is not merely decoration, it's... '

' ...about *terroir*.'

'Yes. *Terroir*. Exactly. The cheese tasted of the pasture on which the animal grazed. Anyway, she was banned from the market, told she was no longer allowed to sell because she did not have a regulation fridge.'

'That doesn't surprise me. It's true that her goats were beautifully groomed. They were dehorned, with hoofs and hair always trimmed and sparkling clean, but I heard the milking space was filthy. And her house... ! She was very, you know *spéciale*.'

I knew that the word special, in French, was far from complimentary.

'I think the neighbours were very happy to see her go.'

'She moved?'

An old man called from the next table. 'We should club together and buy her a regulation fridge!'

A chorus of approval rose up underneath the plane trees.

'But no-one knows where she's gone,' said the first woman.

'What is a regulation fridge?' said a second man.

'I think I've got one in my garage,' said a third.

'Well, we'd better find her,' said the first woman.

I looked at the place where she used to stand, now filled by an eager young man selling photo-shopped images of sunsets over lavender fields. Though I never saw the goat lady again, I have a feeling I have seen her goats.

At first there was nothing out of the ordinary about that particular transhumance, the twice-yearly shunt of sheep and goats between high and low pastures. I was practising, as I remember. I heard the distant clang of bells on leather as the herd wound their way down the mountain path. I kept playing, enjoying their modal accompaniment. The animals came in to view through the window, looking like a string of maggots. They edged their way between the oaks, through the vines, and headed for our hamlet. I went downstairs and mingled with them as they spilled on to our terrace, enveloping me in their woolly carpet. Then I noticed that, unusually, there seemed to be no goats amongst them. I saw the shepherd (who, when he passed our hamlet's sign, regained network coverage after who knows how long) talking animatedly on his mobile phone, but the goats were not with him.

'Look round the corner!' Julian called from the studio window. 'I've got some new fans!'

I looked. A set of three locked horns were knocking against the double-glazed doors at the side of the house. Behind the glass there stood an easel on which a group of small paintings were drying: a lemon, a pomegranate and two landscapes.

'Unfortunately goats are not very well off. Otherwise I might be a rich man!' said Julian.

As I took in the pastoral scene, I couldn't help wondering if there was, on the air, a whiff of lavender, thyme and savory.

Woman in a White Dress

When we started dating six years ago my wife, who is a portrait painter, and I made a deal that if I would start painting, she would take up golf. She bought the clubs, which now lie dormant in the hall closet and I upheld my side of the bargain. I bought one of Julian's portraits.

Joe Stewart, Cincinnati, Ohio, USA

THE SNOW WAS MELTING ON THE VENTOUX and the almond trees, adorned now with papery blossom, were shedding their eerie black fruit. Gradually colour started seeping back into the landscape. Single orchids sprang up from the warm ochre sand, and jonquils and violets appeared on the banks of the tracks. Soon Provence was in glorious bloom and there was no slowing nature's pace as pink and white petals fell, making way for red fruit on a deepening emerald backcloth. There was far too much out there to paint. Missing a day often meant missing a whole crop, so violently could the mistral tear and wither it. In the tug of abundance, the apple on Adam's ex still life remained, along with the portraits of the neighbour's kids, and the house on Long Island, unfinished because the season of plein air painting had begun!

Occasionally, like an unexpected day of sunshine in England, the rain would come, heavy and unapologetic, flowing in under the door and drenching sturdy floorcloths. It was on one such day that Julian did the second portrait of me, and that I failed yet again to ask the question.

I stood in the entrance to the makeshift studio where, for two hours, Julian had been moving a piece of garlic around a frying pan in a sawn-off Birkenstock box.

'Remember that lady with the organic room who wanted celeriac robes?' he said. 'This one is hers but the garlic is just too pink.'

'We could watch an old movie?' I said.

'There's a lovely reflection of the raffia coils in the skillet, though,' he said, keeping his eye upon the set up, 'and the lilac streaks in the bulb could be fabulous with that hint of rose in the copper.'

He hummed a little. Several beginnings, as far as I could tell, from June Tabor's album Apples with the hiccup of the accordion down pat. I watched him drape a pink scarf over the box, take it down, add a week-old baguette crust, subtract it, move an empty bottle of 1959 Chateau Rayas away and place a gold rimmed saucer under the garlic. I left him to it.

He came downstairs forty minutes later.

'Would you like to sit for a portrait?'

'Not if you're going to thrust a knife at me again,' I said.

Julian promised he wouldn't, and together we climbed the stairs back to the studio. I made a trail through the still life debris toward the sitter's chair beneath the window stained with raindrops. 'How do you want me?'

Julian and his easel inhabited the only other available space in the room, inches in front of me. He kicked some kitchen paper from underneath his feet and scraped an area of his palette clear with a blade. He reached up on top of a cupboard and brought down a handful of dusty green fleece material. 'In this hat,' he said.

Julian fiddled with the position and height of the chair, the lights and the background. He placed a book under my forearm to bring the level up, and an old wine box under the back legs of the chair to tilt my head down. Under the hat my hair was scrunched back, with the exception of a few strands he had pulled forward. Then he asked me to focus on his left eye. Lulled by the brushed Morse code of his strokes, I watched his eye changing, becoming a fish darting across the bowl of his glasses, the creases on his skin becoming the tail and fins. Above the eye, his hair was like swirls of seaweed whilst below, the shipwreck of his nose collapsed onto his cheekbone. He measured the proportions of my face with his paintbrush, placing the empty cube of his forefinger and thumb across the frame of his glasses. He nudged a bit of black across to the red on his palette and added some white, peaking it to make a chocolate coloured drop. The eye-fish was finally still. He had found his focus. I wondered if I would dare look at anyone else this frankly.

We had been silent a long while save for his occasional cursing of Winsor and Newton, and now, apparently, he was adding the final touches and starting to relax. He scooped the new hue up onto the tip of the brush and it curtsied onto the canvas.

'I love you,' I said.

'I know. I love you too.'

'Do you?'

'That's the difference between us.'

'What?'

'You don't even know yet that I do.'

Julian pulled a finer brush from the collection of six in his left hand like an arrow from its quiver. 'You're a good sitter.'

'Am I?'

'There you go again. Try not to smile for a sec… '

I did my ventriloquist's best not to move my mouth while Julian tried to explain what he meant about being a good sitter. He said that, because I was not vain (well, I was vain in that I like being painted, and applauded, but that was different) he knew I didn't need him to make me look pretty. I could feel my jaw tighten in to a grimace.

'That's nice,' he said.

The brush strokes had become silent now. Our cat, Oscar, jumped up out of the box of paints where he always slept and on to Julian's lap. Julian scratched the top of his head with a free finger. 'I said, don't smile!'

'But we can't have two depressed portraits.'

'Mm, that's a lovely bit of orange just there on your chin. Yes, that's it.'

It was getting cold. Unlike the artist in his seven layers, I did not have special undergarments to protect me from the chill of the spring evening. I shivered. While Julian continued his monologue I wondered if this might be the moment to ask the question.

'There's a lovely triangle just there,' said Julian. 'This bit and the shadow make a wonderful pattern… the way your hair draws your cheekbone.'

I watched my husband's strong hands at work. He was humming the theme from the kids' show Playschool. He was happy. A wave of nausea rose at the memory of Monsieur Bigonnet informing us he had tied my fallopian tubes while I was under anaesthetic, and most of all at the injustice of this lovely man being denied a chance at fatherhood. Except, of course, there was an alternative, and I was thinking about it more and more often.

'What do you think about…?' I said.

'Not now, darling. I'm busy,' said Julian.

We fell back into silence.

'Don't frown,' said Julian.

At last his brushes clicked for the last time. He unclipped the painting to show me.

'My eyes are too small and I look about seventy.' I said.

'I take it back. You're as vain as the rest of them! I'll put it up as today's postcard. What shall we call it? Her Squinty Highness The Old Bag?'

Julian snatched the last light to photograph the painting. As had become his habit at this point in the day, he poured himself a pastis and changed from classical to folk music, this time singing along at full volume. '*I'm going to do it all someday.*' He sat down at the computer, posted the little portrait entitled Head of a Woman on his site and sent it off to his mailing list.

'About the thing,' he said, 'we'll talk about it sometime, Ruthie. Just not today. You know, about our life... I'm good. I'm having fun.'

Daffodils in a Jam Jar

In cracked jugs and old sinks, in baskets and discarded chimneypots where soot once spouted, and high above the crazy urban life spinning below on Deptford High Street, yellow trumpets dance boldly in the weak sunlight. Soon they will wilt and die, but I shall not cry, because inside, a painting of three daffodils in a humble jam jar will keep them alive.

Carol Grimes, jazz singer and writer, Folkestone, UK

I LAID OUT SEVEN CARDS, one for each day of the coming week, on five mismatched espresso cups and two milk bottle tops. I smoothed down the edges of the boards with sand paper, dipped the brush in gesso and moved the paint around. A pair of golden orioles had started to nest in the plane tree behind the house and, although they rarely gave us a glimpse of their yellow coats, I could listen for hours to the canticle and squawk of their call. Even though we would light a fire that evening, the spring sun beat down on my bare shoulders. A cat curled around my calf and for a moment, all was calm. Then Julian, anxious to start the daily painting, danced on to the terrace, whisked the first board away to the kitchen to dry with a hairdryer and, whilst the machine whirred in his hand, called out a shopping list.

'Lemons. They must be lemony, but not too pale and not lumpy. Not that orange yellow. The ones from Nice with the leaves are normally fine, but hmm, it depends. With the blue box... ' He had recently found some new objects to paint in the antiques market at L'Isle-sur-la-Sorgue. A bone-handled knife, a small crystal glass with a gold rim, a wide-lipped bottle, a silver napkin ring and a gorgeous blue tin box that would soon feature in a whole series of still life paintings.

'A goat's cheese. Has to be tall. Not flat. Not ridged. A *pélardon* if possible.'

'Pretty label?' I asked.

'Label not important. Or a wedge of hard cheese but with good rind.'

'Hang on,' I said, 'let me grab a pen.'

'Those nice *oignons doux de* ...you know, that place. The white papery ones. But they must sit. Strawberries if they are in yet. Not the nice tasting ones from the woods but the big cheap ones. The redder the better. With interesting stalks obviously. Heart shaped and they must sit. Apples if they still have them. Remember, not too much red. Not green. Just enough blush.'

Julian paused to hum. Still Playschool.

I wrote MUST SIT on the back of a telephone bill.

'Soon it will be cherries. Then plums but they never keep their bloom. The film that is so pretty seems to disappear if you as much as look at them. Did you throw away the oyster shells from last night?'

'No. Peas are in season... '

'Peas don't work. Damn. I need a vase. It's ridiculous I don't have a vase. I suppose I could use a jam jar.'

More Playschool. He had been humming it for so long that childhood memories were starting to surface. Now, for example, I was remembering someone in flared trousers

saying: 'This is a green jelly! Do you think it will come out?'
I wondered if the apples on the shopping list had set off the
same apple-flavoured jelly Playschool memory in Julian.

'Mm. Bread!' said Julian. 'A baguette, not that healthy
stone ground stuff. Not too thin. One to paint and two to
eat.'

'But—'

'You've got a problem with bread. It's only eighty cents
for Christ's sake. Buy ten. We can always throw them away.
And *la ratte* potatoes and a pomegranate with a good crown.'

I finished the boards' first coat, rummaged in Julian's
painty trousers for the car keys and was just about to leave
when he shouted from the window.

'Actually. Forget the rest. I've got an idea. Could you get
me some daffodils?'

Postcard

*My interest in France began at an early age with the slides
my father used to show us from Versailles, where he was
stationed in 1952. Not only was my father assigned as
guard to General Omar Bradley and his family in France,
but he was also the sole US Army representative to appear
on a joint French, British and American postcard!*

Vicki Simmons, West Seneca, New York, USA

'NO DAFFODILS,' said the local florist in Bedoin. 'Next week, when it is Grandmother's day, we will have plenty. Can you come back then?'

In the wholesale shop in Carpentras there were bulbs in flower but they came in an obligatory frosted glass vase with a crinkle top. I reserved them and drove further afield to Avignon where I found bulbs without the obligatory vase but they were not the creamy colour Julian wanted. I bought them just in case. Then I moved on to *Botanic* where I found paler daffodils and clusters of creamy narcissi too. I bought those. I drove back to Carpentras where I unreserved the bulbs in the vase, and back home to Bedoin.

'Perfect!' said Julian, and climbed the stairs to his studio.

I applied the silky gesso a second time and placed the boards back on their various receptacles to dry in the sun.

After my excursion, I was looking forward to seeing one of them being host to a daffodil painting. I set up the cutting board, computers, labels, boards and envelopes in preparation for packing up the ten paintings that had sold that month. I loved looking at the addresses, wondering about what kind of houses the paintings would end up in on Ocean Boulevard, Brie Brie Crescent, Burr Avenue or Caverno, Faith or Whispering Pines Drives, and in whose lives in Boca Raton, Baton Rouge, Liberty Hill, Tring or Coon Valley. I cut, folded and taped. I got out the black marker and started to write. Moonee Ponds, Pontypool, Cocoa, Mystic. I allowed my hand to flourish. Block Island, Broken Arrow, Flower Mound, Guelph. The four lines on each package were beginning to feel like odes to people and places I dreamed of visiting.

Later in the day, toward the end of my cello practice, I listened with one ear for the explosion from silence into humming that indicated not only the end of Julian's work day, but how he felt about the daffodil painting he would soon show me. Every day this was a nerve racking moment. In fact, since the launch of Postcard from Provence, every moment of the day was kind of nerve wracking as each one took on a certain quality dependent on where Julian was in relation to his daily painting. The moment when he started work, for example, ranged from a few minutes after his rising to a few minutes before the sun set. 'I'll start early today.' he would say at eight o'clock. 'Try and do a couple. That will give me time at the weekend to work on the portraits. Or I could have a day off and we could go out to LUNCH!'. He might indeed start work early, but more often than not he would hover, and the hovering could last for hours. If I was working he would wander aimlessly into my room. He wouldn't have anything to say. No papers to get nor book to check. He would just stand there. Other distractions were readily available on his computer, of course. The Guardian newspaper on line was particularly riveting that day, and there were the increasing number of daily painter blogs to read. And there was the pantry. There was a carcass in the fridge and stock to be made, or even better, meat to be marinaded or a cake to be created. We had recently discovered home-made lemonade. I might hear the stoking of a fire, the toaster popping, milk being foamed for a third coffee, eggs being beaten or a YouTube video being played. It was all part of the preparation he would say. When Julian did start work (which, after all, was what he wanted to do, and what he now eventually did every day) an exquisite peace fell upon the house.

I could hear the end-of-day humming now. If he had scrubbed a canvas and given up, the hum would be a disjointed dirge, and if he had, as he called it 'done a cracker!', it would be more melodic. This was, I believe—I put down my bow—yes, it was melodic! In fact it was positively boppy! I tried to identify the tune as if that would give me a further clue. Had he had a good day? Because, after all, a good day meant a happy evening together.

'I've done a cracker!' he said, bouncing in to the kitchen. He had the curl of a tangerine peel perched on his head for extra effect and was holding a small painting in his hand.

I looked at the painting, crestfallen. 'Where are the daffo... ?'

'Don't you like it?'

The daily painting was not of flowers. Nor was it of a bone handled knife, a silver napkin ring or a blue tin. It was of a postcard. A portrait of a young girl by Lucien Freud he kept pinned to his easel. He hopped to the fridge and opened a bottle of white wine.

'Don't worry, I'll paint the daffodils tomorrow!'
'They'll wilt,' I said.
'Don't be such a smelly,' said Julian.

Although I receive a daily email from Julian I don't know the taste of his teacups; what smells his house absorbs and releases or how he feels to hug. Ours is a fragile, two-dimensional friendship, rectangular, like a postcard.

Zinnia, funeral celebrant, London, UK

La Calanque de Sormiou

Until recently, I sat in a beige cube with beige carpeting and mostly beige people, where the arrival of the postcard each day took me to someplace I'd rather be. Now I have an office with a window and a sliver of the river and a horizon between glass and limestone skyscrapers but with the postcards I still get to armchair travel every day,.

Tracy Dale, librarian, Jersey City, New Jersey, USA

TWO OR THREE of each week's postcard paintings were selling now. The still lifes seemed particularly popular and Julian was starting to get emails requesting copies of this one or that, for Cecilia because apricots made her think of her grandmother's jam, for Betty because she used to have a favourite frock embroidered with cherries, or from Thérèse to Sam because she had proposed to him in a leap year over baked aubergine soufflé. On this particular day, however, Julian was in the mood for landscapes and he suggested a trip to the highest sea-cliffs in Europe, for a working mini-break. I protested that I had to figure out what all the crosses and squiggles were in the score that had just arrived in the post, that it was all very well driving down to Marseille but I couldn't practise the cello in a boat.

'Study your score looking out to sea,' said Julian.

In the boot of the car we threw an easel, paints, four gessoed boards, a camera, walking boots, two litres of Badoit, an iPod and the cello part of a Rameau opera, and drove southwards.

After a lunch of grilled sea bass perched high on the one of the calanques, Julian set up under the shade of an umbrella pine overlooking the port of Sormiou. He unfolded his easel, lodging its feet in a bed of needles, pinned his board to it with a clothes-peg, spread his paint tubes out on a rock, and started a seascape. I, meanwhile, propped myself up against the tree's trunk and, inhaling the smells of salt and pine, set about deciphering the hieroglyphics of French baroque ornamentation. Occasionally, as we worked, we pinched ourselves, and recalled the English seaside resorts of our childhood.

'We used to stop on the way down to Bognor at some National Trust house or castle,' said Julian, adding a blob of pale green which made a pine tree leap into the foreground. 'We would pile out of the car and stand peering through the gates. Can we go in? one of us would inevitably ask. No, our dad would say. It's too expensive. You can see it from here. He would then buy a round of 'ninety-nine' cones from the Mr Whippy ice cream van for each of us five kids. I guess this cost him less than one entrance fee, and of course adults didn't have to accompany children eating ice-creams like they had to accompany children walking round castles, and so we would eat our ice creams looking at the posh house through the gates. The we would get back in the car and drive on.'

'We used to go and visit my Nana and Grandad in... '

'Oh no, I've just made that pine tree look like a busby hat!'

'... in a caravan park on the coast at Hastings. I remember having to dress for dinner at the bowls club, and having photos taken of us on the beach in our silky too-grown-up clothes that Nana made with a parrot on each of our shoulders, and looking so silly but just being so happy I didn't have to practice the cello for once....'

'Oh, this is crap. I'm such a fraud. The three-year-old me could have painted this! You see we are living a dream, but the problem is that it's actually a nightmare. What people don't seem to realize is that most of the time painting is a nightmare, I'm a nightmare... '

'Not today though, surely?'

Julian had wiped one board clean and was now easing into a second. His thin-lipped frustration relaxed and he was dabbing playfully at the easel.

'So what's next?' I said, 'Postcard from Bali?'

'Well, certainly not Postcard from Bognor.'

Julian finished the second painting, and did a third, and a fourth just before the rocks started to turn pink in the setting sun. We packed up and made our way home. As the light started to fade on the spacious Highway of the Sun, Julian pulled into a lay-by. He took his boards, now covered with Mediterranean seascapes, placed them on the trunk of the car and photographed them ready to post on the internet that evening. He sold them within an hour of our return.

'A typical day at the office,' Julian said, laughing as we slid underneath the sheets.

'Another bloody nightmare,' I said and turned out the light, knowing our day full of sea air would send us straight to sleep.

Pêche Blanche

My still life is of a peach on a white tea towel with a blue stripe, and a bottle green jug. It hangs now in my office, sharing a wall with a still life by an early California artist named J. Bond Francisco who was part of the plein air school out here. His is of an old cigar box, a tobacco pouch, a pipe, a box of matches with a few used match sticks lying around, and an earthenware jug. The two seem to fit together.

Larry Gilson, Los Angeles, California, USA

THIERRY, A LOCAL BUILDER, was free to put in a concrete floor for us that would apparently stop our house falling down. He had prepared a quote that, once signed and returned, would become a binding contract, and we had decided to approach the bank for a loan. The conversation did not go well.

'*Bonjour Madame. Je m'appelle Madame Ruth Merrow-Smith. Je voudrais...*'

'*Je souhaiterais.*' The bank clerk corrected me.

I tried to explain that we would like to have a loan to do some work on our house, but I was interrupted again.

'Madame Rut, could you...'

I cringed. Unfortunately the French pronunciation of

my name meant animals fucking.

' ...give me your account number, please?'

I was starting to shake at the prospect of the approaching numbers, dreading the part where I had to times twenty by four and add ten plus nine. I looked up at the wall on which hung a quiet painting of a peach on a white tea-cloth with a blue stripe. I tried to bring my mind back to the mathematical task but found myself thinking instead about an email that Julian had received recently in which a lady named Nancy asked where she could find such a 'French cloth'. She wanted, she said, to 'sew a long loop to fit over a wooden dowel' and in the fabric shops she had visited they hadn't seen such 'towelling' in many years. What, I wondered, was a wooden dowel? And should I write to her to say the tea-cloths were ordered on the Internet, made from finest Irish linen and shipped from County Clare?

'Madame Merrow?' The clerk's voice was haughty.

'*Soixante-six, huity-huit...* ' I said.

'*Huit à Huit?*' said the clerk, obviously amused by the accidental mention of the French equivalent to 7-11, the local supermarket that claimed to be open every day from eight to eight but actually closed for three hours at lunch time and then again well in time for the hour of the aperitif.

I started again, number by number: 'six, five, eight, eight, seven, three, nine, nine,' only to find that by the time I reached the end, the clerk had hung up on me.

'Let me try.' Julian who, despite his lack of vocabulary, always managed to make himself understood, especially by women, dialled the number.

'Hello, I am Madame Buffet,' said Madame Buffet. 'What can I do for you?'

Julian explained our situation. Madame Buffet replied that for a loan we would need our *certificats de naissance,* officially translated of course, our *fiches d'imposition* for the last five years, our *acte de vente*, an *extrait du casier judiciaire* for each one of us, an *attestation morale* from the mayor, two *cartes d'identité*, our *bulletins de salaire*, and our *certificat de mariage*. And, of course the bank could only lend us 10 percent of our monthly income.

'What is your monthly income?' said Madame Buffet.

Julian told her.

'A loan?' said Madame Buffet. 'On these figures? Do you take me for an imbecile?'

Abandoned House with Poppy Field

I receive Postcards from Provence on my laptop at the long farmhouse table where I write copy in my Hackney lower-ground kitchen, looking out onto a middlingly gritty inner-city terraced street with two acacia trees and a cockerel. However, the home where I spent my childhood holidays is only a few miles from the ruined hamlet of Les Couguieux, so I always wonder if I can recognize the views. I'm afraid I rarely can!

Sophie Dening, journalist and editor, London, UK

NICE SPOT!' Adèle called down from her horse, her boots shiny in the sun. We had met her recently through a bow maker whom we knew through a potter in the village. 'By the way, you've got some whopper cracks in your façade.'

'We know,' I called back, not grateful for the reminder. 'We are just about to put a concrete floor in to stabilise... '

Adèle pulled in her reins and jabbed the horse's ribs with her heel. The animal halted and she jumped off. She said we couldn't put concrete in an old stone house, that it was tantamount to putting it in a human body. It blocked the house's chi. She said we should look into hemp. It was related to the marijuana plant, which was why, she continued, despite its potential to provide not only clothes, banknotes, bibles, ropes and building materials, but also energy, it had been outlawed in the US in 1937. 'And did you know refusing to grow it was illegal for the three previous centuries? George Washington and Thomas Jefferson grew it. Van Gogh and Rembrandt painted on it. I will introduce you to Yves who builds with it. He'll change your mind. He changes everyone's mind.' Adèle mounted and kicked her heels into the horse once more and they cantered off.

I inhaled the fresh pat of dung Adèle's horse had left on the roadside and considered how little I had contributed to the environmental cause: in my teens I had worn a CND badge but had refused to lie with my mother across a muddy road in protest against nuclear power. In my twenties I had, despite my copy of What Green Car?, fallen for a Swedish guzzler with a sun roof that I kept open in winter with the heating on full. When I bought my first flat I toyed with Auro organic paints but opted instead for the cheaper Dulux. I didn't bother taking the plastic stoppers out of bottles when I recycled them and I only bought organic apples because they tasted better.

'I had a half-chat with Adèle,' I said as Julian came downstairs holding a bunch of irises, their silken tongues shrivelled with thirst.

'Yes, I saw the Bio Brigade out on horseback. Very good for the planet all that dung. Could you get a word in edgeways?'

'No, not really, but what she was saying sounded interesting.'

'Was she telling you how you could knit cars with Himalayan balsam? She reminds me of a girl I used to date at art school. I don't know what it is about Doc Marten's.'

'No,' I said. 'She was talking about something called hump or hemp or bump or something. She says we should make a bump floor not a concrete one... '

'We can't do that, sweetheart. We're just about to sign Thierry's devis ...well, we will when I get Bernard's dad's bloody irises done. We can't let Thierry down now. He knows what he's talking about, and he said that a thin layer of concrete was the best way to... '

'She was going to send this guy Yves round to take a look. Apparently he's the world expert on bio-dynamic building.'

'When's he coming?'

'Tomorrow, maybe. You only have to turn the pages of *Côté Sud* to see that's it's not only baguettes that are *à l'ancienne* these days. They've been building with these materials for centuries in Morocco... '

'Yeah, and that inspired you to do what? To paint your flat all those weird colours? Like Souk Green and Bargain Rug Purple and Mint Tea With Too Much Sugar God Willing? Anyway, I know all about natural materials as they are pretty much the same as in painting: caseine, lime, wax, rabbit skin glue, ochres, hog bristle, poppy seed, linseed oils and ground precious stones, and I fully intend using them once the concrete floor is in and the house is no longer in danger of crumbling round our ankles. Tell Adèle we'll call Yves when we're ready to decorate.'

'Damn' said Julian, seeing Yves pull up the next afternoon. He threw his brushes in the sink and dragged his feet down the stairs where I was already lapping up the wisdom of the bio guru.

'Good day,' said Yves. His shaved head shone and his frayed hemp waistcoat hung elegantly on his taut body. He sported a designer goatee and his forget-me-not blue eyes were framed by fine wire ovals. He looked like Professor Tournesol. 'Everyone in Hollywood is having a facelift! Is a house, like an aging woman, no longer allowed to grow old?' he said. 'Is she not allowed to have wrinkles? These cracks are her wrinkles!' He held our gaze and continued. 'The house, just like a human body, has a skeletal structure. It has flesh and an epidermis. It is an envelope for the spirit with all the same functions: breath, absorption, insulation, transpiration, and elimination. Just like the human envelope. The old masons knew this, just as they knew how to lay a stone with its feet on the earth and its head toward the heavens.'

Yves continued to hold forth. I remembered hikes in the Lake District, and the poetry of dry stone walling trotted through my head like the lines of a long-forgotten Sunday school poem. Smoot (the hole near the top through which a person could observe game without being seen); bolt hole (near the base through which rabbits could run); cripple hole (through which sheep could pass).

I looked up at our house. A bright lizard was making its way up the mossy crack in the façade toward the crimped hem of the roof tiles, and where the façade was worn the rounded *galets* showed through like knee joints. The butt of the central beam was visible like a last vertebra and a black redstart whooshed into the space above it with a beak full of twiglets. A Mediterranean pine tree nuzzled in to the building's shoulder. Air whistled through the windows and doors with all its gossip and the floors listened. It was, indeed, a living, breathing thing.

'That's why the buildings don't fall down even though the mortar may fall away. If you make a façade with concrete, naturally, because the walls constrict and can no longer breathe, you get damp.'

Yves lay his hand up against the render warmed by the sun with the sensitivity of a lover. Skin on skin.

Bank of Wildflowers

I knew I wanted to be an artist in the eighth grade. We were shopping for groceries in the A&P. I begged my mom to buy me a cardboard print of the Van Gogh sunflowers and I've been in love with the whole tragic story ever since. I am now a member of the plein air painters of Alabama. Working four days a week in marketing I am often too tired to paint, but Julian's work ethic makes me re-examine my excuses.

Amy Echols, marketing director, Tuscaloosa, Alabama, USA

IT WAS THE TIME OF wildflowers, and Bernard was on line again with another purple request.

> From: Bernard@withersanddraper.co.uk
> Subject: more bloody mauve
>
> Now pay attention Julianna. I have mentioned the possibility of a further commission for my Dad. Boring subject... bloody irises. The specimen in question appears at present in his back garden and its friends call it 'Persian Knight' aka iris sibirica. If you are gonna do it I want it done proper, not in this bloody woolly hat style that's been creeping in. Mind you; short season, huh? Might have to be plastic ones. By the way - why is the cat in your painting sleeping on rhubarb?

'Cos she's a sourpuss' replied Julian, adding that he'd have a bash.

WE LAY OUR BICYCLES DOWN by the bank of pale blue irises. These were the last of the season, and if Julian didn't capture them now, Bernard's dad would have to wait another year.

'It is not his words that are compelling,' Julian said as he dismantled the easel and spread the picnic over the grass.

Was he talking about Bernard? Surely he was not talking about Yves?

'What is compelling is his grace.'

It had been several weeks now since the bio-mason's visit and I was sure Julian had thought nothing more of him or his radiant, electromagnetic, biothermic, phonic, sonic building methods. Apparently I was wrong.

'So the spiritual stuff didn't press your ex-Catholic buttons?'

From the bike panniers Julian pulled four old variety tomatoes, the skin of each one spotted and cloven in three. There was crusty rye bread still warm from the bakery, and a bottle of red wine.

'I like the sound of the hemp,' he said. 'We could fill buckets of ochre from down the road to mix with lime for the façade, and we could collect stones on our walks, just like they used to in the old days, to rebuild the walls. Could you imagine, if we could pay Yves to do up the entire hay-loft as a studio?'

'Even if we could pay him, you wouldn't let someone else dismantle a hornet's nest in your own knickers, let alone build you a studio.'

The wall of purple flowers towered above us, the delicate curl of their petals quivering like prayer flags in the remnant of the mistral. The movement seemed to intensify their scent. Julian unpacked a tube of blue from his paint-box.

'Yves is running a course next month,' I said. 'Can I invite you for an early wedding anniversary gift?'

'Sure,' said Julian. 'In fact, I'll knock these off this afternoon for Bernard and that way he can foot the bill instead and you can take me out to lunch for our wedding anniversary!'

Julian and I arrived for the organic building course in a downpour of spring rain. The warehouse, just outside Avignon, was opposite a rape field, and it lay like a slug along the riverbank. Inside, a single bulb hung from the beamed ceiling and an oil heater fumed at the end of the room. Dotted around the space were a couple of half-built walls, a dozen industrial black dustbins, a collection of greyish balls that looked like horse poo, and three hay bales. Since there were no toilets the participants were encouraged to pee in the nearby reed bed before meeting their fellow coursemates. As, one by one, we returned from thus relieving ourselves, we were welcomed with luke warm Rooibos tea and quinoa biscuits.

There were nine other people sharing the refreshments, with whom we would go on to share the weekend. A middle aged hurdy-gurdy player living in a château; a nurse from the Pays Basque with a nest of black hair and her gawky boyfriend; a world-famous soprano in John Deere tractor overalls; a traveller who, in his holy Stetson, looked as if he had walked straight out of Tess of the d'Urbervilles; a man with halitosis who described himself as a 'vegetable sculptor'; a specialist in adobe building from Santa Fe, and a Moroccan stone-mason. The motivations of the group ranged from wanting to save the planet through building a straw house and designing the first hundred percent organic restaurant to simple curiosity.

Yves's introduction, though Julian and I had heard much of it before, was immediately riveting. With hands spiralling, and emphasising his words with a tango step forward or a shuffle to the side, he held forth, his speech studded with trigger words such as 'alchemical,' 'prayer,' 'sacred', 'energy' and 'vibration.' Julian did not leave the room. He wasn't even twitching. In fact, he was mesmerised.

'What's that line from Jerry McGuire?' he said when Yves had finished and was scuffling to the back of the room in search of tools.

'You had me at hello?'

'Yes. He had me at *bonjour*.'

'He had me at '*la maçonnerie c'est la chanson de l'enveloppe de l'âme*.'

'What does that mean?'

'Building is the song of the soul's envelope, or something.'

The group, digesting what it had just heard, sat in stillness and listened to the raindrops, like a thousand baby fingers drumming on goatskin.

'Ok, let's get to work!' Yves said, returning with a palette knife and twirling round to face his awestruck audience.

The mixer chugged and clacked and we whipped up lime, ochre, hemp and pumice. With the mixtures we constructed a baby hemp wall, a stuccoed tile, turned a hay bale into a tadelakt bar and laid a small 'sonic' floor. We mixed red and yellow ochre in huge bins and folded it into creamy lime like chocolate into egg whites in a giant cake mixture. Then we spread it over a surface like icing. We touched, pounded, combed and splat. We smoothed surfaces in silky figures of eight, employing the same sensitivity with which a string player would listen to the vibration of the string through the hair of his bow. We tamped down hemp floors with our bare feet like a troupe of tribal dancers, and by lunch time Julian was as flushed and shiny as the tadelakt surface he had just finished polishing. We all collapsed on to hay bales and delved into baskets and knapsacks, each person producing leaves, cheese, bread, flowers, salad herbs and wine to share. We were the only people who had brought nothing.

Yves kept talking. 'It is like playing a musical instrument,' he said, describing the technique of flicking on the lime primer called gobeti. 'You must not be frightened of large gestures. The movement originates in your centre, like this.'

He got up, took a step back to gather energy, bent his knees, sprang forward and, with his forearm and wrist following through the impulse that clearly came from his solar plexus, flicked some of the pumice and lime mixture on a nearby wall. It landed evenly across the surface with the cocky perfection of the ball at the end of a tennis champion's backhand slice. Then he sat back down, picked up his apple and took a bite.

'I heard he danced with Margot Fonteyn before this,' said one of the participants. 'Then he burned out and went to live with the shepherds in the mountains.'

'I heard he was a sufi,' said another. 'He did some bowing ritual before we started, did you notice?'

'Well, he certainly isn't a Catholic!' said Julian.

Yves got up and was moving toward the centre of the room. People started to gather round him.

'Let's talk about prosperity,' he said. 'We have to do this work in a spirit of prosperity and not fear. To build an envelope for the human spirit is one of the most beautiful things man can do, but it's no use doing beautiful work if you do not trust it will bring riches. You do not know yet whom your work will reach or what form your prosperity will take but you must trust in the creation of it, not just for your-selves but for those around you and for the planet. Right, let's get to work.'

Julian and I returned home blinking with lime dust and emotion.

'Before I can say 'tadelakt," I said as I moved Bernard's dad's painting, packed and ready to post, to one side of the kitchen table, 'you will be going to a male bonding medita-tion sweat lodge!'

'I'm sure Yves sells plenty of marijuana walls and bran flake floors with that line about prosperity. But yes, he cer-tainly has an extraordinary presence, and the materials are wonderfully light to handle. We can't afford to get the mae-stro himself, but I'm up for having a go. When do we start?'

Daffodil on a Tile

In April 2005 I visited Ruth and Julian in the Hameau des Couguieux. *Postcard from Provence* was newly born then, an infant two months old. It was the time of red dots and an abundance of available paintings at $100 apiece.

The evening I arrived we ate something delicious Julian made, and gulped Vacqueyras. We gabbled all the new things we had to say, loud and greedy as geese. By the end of the weekend we'd calmed; the fire was lit, books were opened, cats curled, Joni sang.

I climbed stone stairs to the studio. On a table smeared with paint, hardboard postcards leant in higgledy-piggledy stacks against the wall. I laid them flat and sorted them into fruits and skies, then colours; blues, citruses, aubergine-purples, shuffling until I made happy families.

'You've been up there ages. What are you doing?' called Ruth.

'Just looking,' I said.

I wanted to be alone with the pictures, handling them, sifting, making choices. I didn't want to share the experience of looking at them, even with their creator. Maybe I felt sneaky, as if I was doing something out of bounds like arranging someone else's CDs into my order. Maybe I just didn't want my friends to witness this autistic episode.

I chose an apple as a gift for my grandfather on his

ninetieth birthday. He was a conscientious objector, a clergyman, a painter with watercolour, and I knew he would appreciate the strokes of green and red and some wordless metaphor I saw there. It was his last birthday, and the picture now hangs in my bedroom.

I chose a wild daffodil on a tile for my mother on her sixtieth birthday. It made me think of Vermeer having a dreamy day.

I might have stopped there but this was a one-off kind of shopping experience and two other pictures kept shouting BARGAIN at me. They were large, more like full-blown letters than postcards; one a hanging bunch of shallots, and the other a fat, green Bramley apple.

I took the four pictures down and showed them to Julian hoping that he'd approve of my tasteful choices and think that I was ever so arty-farty. I thought he might say, 'oh no, not the tile and the daffodil—I put my soul into that and I can't bear to see it go.' Instead, I saw the excitement of a sale in his eyes.

Julia Gooding, soprano and cranio-sacral therapist, E.Sussex, UK

Lemon and Orange on a French Cloth

On a visit to Julian's studio, our friend Donna held the postcard-sized paintings in her hands one at a time, murmuring 'I think I can do something with these....'

Johanne Killeen, cook, Providence, Rhode Island, USA

JULIAN HAD THOUGHT NOTHING OF THE MEETING with Jo and George's friend, Donna. The day after the biodynamic building and prosperity weekend, however, he received an email from the journalist.

To:jms@provenceart.com
Subject: careful...

Dear Julian, I sold the article to the New York Times last week and we are running it in tomorrow's edition. Careful what you wish for.

Donna

The next day, at about seven am East Coast Time, Julian decided to go running. A year before, his father had a heart scare and Julian found himself telling him to please exercise just a little bit every day, even if it was walking rather than driving to the village shop. Seeing the irony of a sedentary man of nearly fifty telling a sedentary man of seventy-eight to get out more, Julian had come back from a shopping trip that afternoon with the most expensive pair of Nikes on the market, and had bounced out onto the route that I pounded every day in my three year old Basics. He hadn't been since, however. Until today.

'It was great!' Julian said, returning an hour later, his face blotchy above his soaked tee shirt. 'I felt like I was floating! And my shoes are so beautiful. I've gone twice now which means that each time cost only fifty euros! Next time I go I will have reduced it to thirty three point three three... I'm just off to take a shower and have a shave.'

'No, you're bloody not,' I said. 'There's no time for that. Look at your inbox. It's going bonkers.'

The purchases had started at reasonably well-spaced intervals minutes after Julian had closed the door behind him, and I had sat alone watching what felt like Postcard from Provence going into labour on the screen.

'Why did you have to choose that moment to be absent?' I asked.

Julian looked over at his screen. The orders were coming in thick and fast now.

Fastcard purchase number 24367*****card transaction...
Fastcard purchase number 24368*****card transaction...
Fastcard purchase number 24368*****card transaction...

After a pause, Julian said, 'I had to go out. I couldn't bear to see it being stillborn.'

Julian and I set ourselves up in the living room and tuned both our laptops in to his gmail. There was no time to think. The paintings were being snatched from the 'available' category as eagerly as New Yorkers might snatch the last blueberry muffin from Starbucks. We could hardly cope. Months earlier, Julian had spent several hours hand crafting a 'sold' dot in Photoshop. It was small and carmine red with slightly fuzzy edges. Placing it in the bottom right hand corner of a thumbnail image was a fiddly process involving cutting and pasting, and one intended for the contented artist who had just sold a single painting, but not four hundred. The current payment system also was antiquated and unable to deal with the strain. Multiple sales for a single painting were going through and refunds had to be quick.

'Here comes another one,' I said.

'What is it?'

'Moon and oak tree.'

'That one's just gone. Can you write? I'll dot and refund.'

'I've just googled her. She's a really swish interior decorator in New York.'

'No time for client googling. Can you make a list of all the purchases and the paintings so far?'

During a temporary lull, Julian looked up the article that had generated all this chaos.

'Listen to this. 'A high speed internet connection allows Mr Merrow-Smith to live the slow-paced life of a nineteenth century landscape painter whilst reaching today's global market.''

'What are you on?'

'Just google Julian and New York Times, or Postcard or Provence or Donna Paul and it will come up, but keep an eye on my inbox.'

There, on the screen, was a photograph of Julian in his Renoir tee shirt clutching at a bunch of brushes like a corn dolly. Above it was the orange and lemon on a blue striped French cloth, and the moon and oak tree. I started to read but was immediately interrupted by another sale.

'Look Julian!' I screamed, 'it's Mara Liasson from National Public Radio!!'

'And someone from Marlborough galleries.'

Finally, the swarm of emails thinned out. Though the keys of the two laptops clicked softly on underneath the pads of each of the three fingers we used, between us, to type, there was now only clearing up left to do.

We looked around us. Handwritten lists dashed with crosses, ticks and lines were strewn over the sofa and floor. We tried to take in the fact that Julian had, in two hours, sold every painting he had ever done. Once the postcard paintings had dried up, bigger paintings had started to shift and the walls had been relieved of the weight of old portraits, dusty lavender fields and morning views of the Rhône. There had been requests for portraits of children, wives, dogs and grandmothers, and the offer of a label design for a line of New Mexican chillies. The only painting that remained in the big old house was Adam's ex still life with the unfinished apple in the corner, and the sketch of the house in Long Island.

'Why don't you put Adam's ex up for sale?' I asked when Julian had returned from the garage with a pile of canvasses. 'It's gorgeous. You could finish the apple in a jiffy, I'm sure.'

'Bad vibe. So I'm all sold out. I think we have to change the name of the site from Shifting Light to Shifted Light.'

'Or Shifting Paintings.'

Julian looked out the window. It was pitch dark. He heaved a sigh of relief. 'Or, if it goes on like this, Night Shift. I'm going to write to Hank in Long Island, finally, and tell him I can't do his grandmother's house.'

I arranged the papers covered with New York addresses.

'Well, Mr Badger, it looks to me like your baby is alive and kicking. Congratulations!'

When Julian became a star, we were inspired to create a celebratory drink. It seemed appropriate to use the subjects of Donna's favorite painting: Still Life with Lemon and Orange on a French Cloth.

Johanne Killeen, cook, Providence, Rhode Island, USA

A CHAMPAGNE TOAST TO JULIAN

Champagne
Cointreau
Cognac
Angostura bitters
Slices of orange
Slices of lemon

Fill large wine glasses ¼ full with ice cubes. Pour in 3 to 4 ounces of champagne per serving. Add a splash of Cointreau, a few drops of cognac, and 3 to 4 dashes of Angostura bitters to each glass and gently stir. Garnish with slices of orange and lemon and serve right away. Makes 6 to 8 champagne cocktails.

Night Moon

*On 10 July 2008 Julian posted a painting of the night
moon outside Les Couguieux. That night as I was leaving
my studio, I looked up and was stopped dead in my tracks.
I felt immediately connected to Julian as I was looking at
the same moon and realizing just how close art makes us.
And how small the world really is.*

Stephen Magsig, artist, Ferndale, Michigan, USA

I DON'T KNOW WHAT IT IS ABOUT SPEEDING, but Julian
had the ball of his foot once more heavily planted on the
gas pedal (this time not going round the London orbital,
but cruising down Provence's 'Sunshine Highway') when he
proposed to me for the second time.

It was May. It was, as Julian had always promised it
would be, glorious, and Provence was indeed infused with
colour and scent. In the Marchés de Provence, the season
of cardoons and potatoes was but a distant memory. The
words *Espagne* and *Tunisie* had been replaced on the labels
of strawberries, melons, broad beans, peas and peaches with
du pays. From here. Blushing apricots nestled in boxes, and
ancient varieties of tomato leered from shelves, inviting
cooks to partner their sweet flesh with grassy olive oil. On
the roadside, banks of poppies were lit up by the acid green

of spurge like inverted crêpe lanterns.

Meanwhile, in le Hameau des Artistes, painting sales had doubled and I was starting to play more locally. A concert at Chateau Rayas had been paid, in part, in wine. Madame Bellon had come to hear me play at a private soirée in Crillon le Brave, and a modest festival had started up in Carpentras (in which, incidentally, I found myself playing with a clarinettist who made reeds for a certain firm called D'Addario). We had thrown away the budget quote for the concrete floor and had contracted Yves to build Julian's studio. The mailing list that only six months earlier had consisted of three names had now reached two hundred, and Julian was receiving comments from as far as Australia:

Every day I sit in my office in this dreary wet town in winter and I open my mail to see your daily Postcard of Provence in the summer. Every day it warms me up and makes me smile.

... and as near as two hamlets away:

Dear Monsieur, the house you have today painted is the house I live in since I am a boy. I am a great admirer of your work and am myself artist-painter. I hope you will come and have the aperitif in this house with my wife and myself. Please excuse my bad English I am Provençal through to the very bone.

We had dropped Julian's parents off at Marseille airport and were driving north back toward Avignon in silence. Despite the abundance of new growth around us, and even a real sense of approaching prosperity, we were feeling the impermanence of things, our unit of two suddenly vulnerable.

Margaret, nervous about the flight, had been particularly fragile when we said goodbye, and I think we were all aware it might be one of her last visits to us. Indeed, though we did have one more Christmas together (for which Julian actually finished the fireplace) Julian's mother died the following winter. Julian was humming a bit. A nursery rhyme, I think. Or was it the theme tune to Andy Pandy? His melancholy rendition of the chirpy tune made me think of Schubert's knack of making the major key seem even sadder than the minor. To distract ourselves, we occasionally read signs out loud together.

'Assoler?' I was looking at a billboard for a garden store. 'What the bloody hell is that?'

'It means crop rotation.'

What was I thinking when he asked? I was thinking about Margaret's smile after her lavender oil facial. I was thinking that Julian was a man who, when he tried to form a phrase in French such as 'Please could you give me two paint tubes and a brush?' would replace both objects with the word for thing—please could you give me two things and a thing?— and so how the hell did he know the word for crop rotation? I was thinking Julian was the only one of the children not to have given Margaret and Hugh grand-children and wondering if they were sad about this. Then I was trying to imagine how exactly one would pronounce assoler without causing offence, when—bang! Out of the clear blue sky it came.

'Ruthie,' said Julian. He pressed his foot down a little harder on the gas and I could hear him swallowing an involuntary verse of something. For an instant, he took both hands off the wheel. Then he put them back, took a quick look at me and looked back at the road. 'What about this adoption idea?'

'Yes!' I said. The word that had been waiting three years to escape was overeager and I wanted to take it back, clear my throat, and say it again in a grown-up voice. I tried to speak slowly. 'Yes? What about it?'

'I'm up for it. It's wonderful, our life, but now I want to share it. I want to share all this... ' Julian waved his hand in the manner of Monsieur Chauvet, indicating the wealth of beauty, of 'motif' as my father once called it, that was outside the window.

'I want to share it with you...'

I followed his gesture and saw the muscular blue shadows of the Montagne Sainte-Victoire rise up ahead of us. A puff of clouds floated on its shoulders like a feather boa.

' ...and I also want to share it with a child.'

Balsamic Bottle, Jug and Shallot

Given to us on the eve of our wedding. I, the pregnant milk jug, lean in to the balsamic blessing of husband and father to be. A small mute shallot awaits her time...

This is the most profound gift of my life. Having arrived, after years of anguish, mourning and forgiveness, at this extraordinary place of simplicity and love, I am acknowledged and embraced in this song without words, this utterly lovely painting.

Julian's painting warms our kitchen wall— it couldn't go anywhere else than the hub of our family life! And not a day goes by without me or a visitor coming into this room and celebrating it, because when something is truly beautiful, whatever the culture or method, we all recognise that beauty in ourselves. It connects us again, it unifies, just like the marriage which its creation first blessed.

Sophie Harris, cellist, London, UK

Pinasses on the River Niger

*When I discovered Shifting Light we were completing the
final stages of an overseas adoption, going down to Haiti
to pick up our son and then being told that there was
another snag and that we couldn't take him home. The
daily paintings felt like a lifeline, a gift that turned anxiety
in to peace, calm and sheer beauty.*

Eric Shapiro, money manager, Boston, Massachusetts, USA

JOSEPH'S HOUSE is made entirely from mud, rice and *beurre
de karité*. We lie on its roof, watching the stars being swallowed, one by one, by the morning. A lizard, flesh-pink and
sporting a black-and-white tuxedo, pauses on a parapet to
perform a series of hurried press-ups. Below us, in the open
grids of the compounds, families pass the time before they
are called to prayer. In each square someone is washing,
grain-sifting, mango-eating, millet-pounding, singing, cora-
playing or baby-rocking. As the silver disc of the sun slices
into the sky we hear the call of the muezzin. It rises and falls,
and folds in upon itself, as if the very pitch were prostrating
to Allah. The doors of Djenné's mosque beckon. Gradually
the grids below us empty and the barely guttered streets fill.
Men in soft bogolan and shiny cotton tunics stream down
them. Women with wraparound pagnes and headdresses

stiff and high as meringues march proud alongside shit-filled drains. Boys descend from ladders where they are plastering buildings with mud and rice husks, joining the throng of young girls carrying small boys on their backs, and small boys carrying babies. The children kick the black plastic bags that litter the mud streets as if they were autumn leaves. There is so much laughter. The mosque fills, the muezzin stops and then there is silence.

'What do you think about Joshua?' says Julian in the sudden hush.

We are racked with dysentery and mangoed-out. Farther south, on a desk on the fourth floor of an office building behind the river Niger, in the sixth commune of Mali's capital, Bamako, there sits a dossier. A beautiful hand-crafted dossier stating, in Helvetica, our continuing desire for a family.

'Agnes?' I say. 'That was my mad grandmother's name, but it's nice in French.'

'Lily?' he says.

'Samuel?' I say.

'Gabriel?' he says.

'Joni?' I say. 'After our favourite...'

'Oh,' he says, 'what I would give for fish and chips with crispy batter on the West Coast of Scotland with a pint of...'

'Lucien? After your favourite...'

'Red Cuillin. Buttercup? Mmm... Heinz tomato soup. I don't know what it is about this harmattan.'

'Harry? Marty?'

'Ruthie, I think we will have to see who comes to us before we give our child a name.'

I look across to the mosque. The ostrich eggs atop its spires that symbolize fertility and purity barely shiver in the first whisper of the desert wind. Below, a woman crosses the square and climbs the three wide steps to the main entrance. Her bare heels are pale as they spring away from the earth. Her neck flows upwards into the dusty sky. Her hips are so perfectly aligned carrying the extra weight of the child that she seems to be floating to the sound of a gentle inner music. As she slips in through the door she turns and looks up, and in that moment I feel a thread weaving its way from her toward us. A thread that is part of a net, at every node of which faces appear like jewels, reflecting all the other faces.

'Grace?' I say.

Acknowledgements

Sometimes an angel appears in your life for no reason. Viqi, I can never thank you enough. This book would not exist without you. Thank you also to Kate, Leo, Fiona, Morgan and Jim for your time, encouragement and friendship. To everyone on the mailing list who took the time to write to me, I raise a full glass. All your stories are part of this book, even if they do not appear here. Above all, thank you to my beloved Julian. You continue, every day, to teach me how to see.

RP, Les Couguieux, 2011

About the Author

Ruth Phillips is a cellist. She lives with her husband, the painter Julian Merrow-Smith, in Provence. This is her first book.

Also by Red Ochre Press:

POSTCARD FROM PROVENCE
Paintings by Julian Merrow-Smith
ISBN number 9782953450002

Praise for the project Postcard from Provence:

'Merrow-Smith...lives the slow paced life of a 19th Century landscape painter while reaching today's global market' - *New York Times*

'Beautiful and evocative...' - *The Times*

'Perfect little pictures of vegetables from his garden or fruit from the market, and luminous, ever-changing Provençal landscapes' - *The Guardian*

Lightning Source UK Ltd.
Milton Keynes UK
UKOW02f0913150916

283039UK00002B/17/P